THE PEASANT WAR
BY

E. Belfort Bax

The Peasant War

Preface

In presenting a general view of the incidents of the so-called Peasants War of 1525, the historian encounters more than one difficulty peculiar to the subject. He has, in the first place, a special trouble in preserving the true proportion in his narrative. Now, proportion is always the crux in historical work, but here, in describing a more or less spontaneous movement over a wide area, in which movement there are hundreds of different centres with each its own story to tell, it is indeed hard to know at times what to include and what to leave out. True, the essential similarity in the origin and course of events renders a recapitulation of the different local risings unnecessary and indeed embarrassing for readers whose aim is to obtain a general notion. But the author always runs the risk of being waylaid by some critic in ambush, who will accuse him of omitting details that should have been recorded.

Again, the approximate simultaneity of the risings over a wide extent of territory makes it impossible to preserve chronological sequence in the general survey. Yet again, here, even more than elsewhere, discrepancies are to be found in different accounts of the same event, and the historian, writing for the general reader, must either reconcile them to the best of his power or choose between them. He cannot well give a wealth of variorum versions or enter into elaborate disquisitions justifying the view he takes, To do either would change the character of such a work as this from a volume designed for the average reader of history to a dissertation for the benefit of a specialist student of Reformation history.

I mention these difficulties as there is always a field in a work of this nature for the ingenuity of a hostile reviewer qui cherche les puces dans la paille to hunt out minutiae on which two opinions may be held. By enlarging upon them, he attempts to disparage the work as a whole. A former volume, dealing with German Society in Reformation times, received favourable recognition, I believe, in every quarter save one. The one hostile review appeared anonymously in a literary journal, which, if I mistake not, was then making a special point of signed reviews. Internal evidence identified the critic as a gentleman who has been believed, rightly or wrongly, to have been for some years preparing material for a work on German Reformation History. Of the somewhat laboured attempts in the article in question to prove the inadequacy of my book, I will only mention one. Quoting a narrative passage, the reviewer stigmatised it as in the style of Zimmermann, which, he observes, "belongs to an obsolete method of writing history". Now, Zimmermann's method was to bring an historical event, as realistically as his power of language would go, before the mind's eye of the reader. This method our superfine and would-be up-to-date critic describes as obsolete! I need only point out that, if so, the late Professor Freeman and the late Mr. J. R. Green, not to speak of other .leading historians, English and foreign, must be reckoned as exceedingly "obsolete" persons. That Zimmermann possessed in an exceptional degree the gift of such descriptive writing has been remarked by all who have read him. Personally, I make no claim to the power, and do not wish to excuse my own shortcomings, but I can only say that if such writing be obsolete, the sooner it be revived the better. Surely the faculty of reproducing the past as a living present remains the ideal of historical literary style!

The literature of the Peasants War is considerable in German-speaking countries. An immense amount of exceedingly careful research has been applied to the collection and elucidation of documents relating to the movement in different places and districts. Just as in Paris there are many retired scholars whose hobby it is to spend their lives in collecting every scrap of information concerning the French Revolution and the lives of the actors in it, so here, although perhaps on a smaller scale, there are many German bibliophiles who have devoted years to investigating in elaborate detail the facts in connection with the events and persons of the 1525 revolt. Instead of cumbering the text with a multitude of footnotes, I give here a list of some principal authorities consulted:-

Zimmermann's Allgemeine Geschichte des grossen Bauernkrieges.

Do., 1891 edition, edited by Wilhelm Blos.

Bezold's Geschichte der deutschen Reformation.

Janssen's Geschichte des deutschen Volkes.

Egelhaaf's Deutsche Geschichte im 16ten. Jahrhundert.

Lamprecht's Deutsche Geschichte.

Ranke's Deutsche Geschichte im Zeitalter der Reformation.

Weill's Der Bauernkrieg.

Hartfelder's Geschichte des Bauernkrieges in Süddeutschland.

Amongst the collection of contemporary documents and early sources that have been found useful may be mentioned:-

Sehreiber's Der deutsche Bauernkrieg gleichseitige Urkunden.

Baumann's Akien zur Geschichte des deutschen Bauernkrieges aus Oberschwaben.

Zimmersche Chronik.

Villinger Chronik.

Rothenburger Chronik.

Schwabisch Hall, Chronika, etc.

Sebastian Franck's Chronik.

Melancthon's pamphlet on Thomas Münzer, and other documents in Luther's Sämmtliche Werke.

Tagebuch des Herolds Hans Lutz von Augsburg, published from the original manuscript in

Zeitschrift für die Geschichte des Oberrheins.

Lorenz Fries's Geschichte des Bauernkrieges in Ostfranken.

Gotz von Berlichingen's Lebensbeschreibung.

Haarer's Eigentliche Warhafftige Beschreibung dess Bawrenkriegs.

The various pamphlets by Thomas Münzer.

Amongst monographs on special subjects connected with the events of 1525 may be mentioned :-

The chapters relating to the revolt in Thuringia, by Kautsky, in the Geschichte des Sozalismus, Band i.

Seidemann's Thomas Münzer.

Blos's Pater Ambrosius.

Barthold's Georg von Frundsberg.

I give the above partial list to obviate the inconvenience of crowding up the text with references. Of all the works on the Peasants War, that of Zimmermann still holds the first place, alike for comprehensiveness of view and accuracy. Many details, it is true, have been corrected and expanded by later research, but empathetic understanding of the movement, historical insight, Zimmermann yet hardly been equalled and certainly not surpassed.

To render the present volume complete, a map of Reformation-Germany (from Spruner-Menke's Historischer Atlas has been included.

E. B. B.

Chapter I. The Situation During the First Quarter of the Sixteenth Century.

In a former volume(1) we considered at length the condition of Central Europe at the close of the period known as the Middle Ales. It will suffice here to recapitulate in a few paragraphs the general position.

The time was out of joint in a very literal sense of that somewhat hackneyed phrase. Every established institution — political, social, and religious — was shaken and showed the rents and fissures caused by time and by the growth of a new life underneath it. The empire — the Holy Roman — was in a parlous way as regarded its cohesion. The power of the princes, the representatives of local centralised authority, was proving itself too strong for the power of the emperor, the recognised representative of centralised authority for the whole German-speaking world. This meant the undermining and eventual disruption of the smaller social and political unities,(2) the knightly manors with the privileges attached to the knightly class generally. The knighthood, or lower nobility, had acted as a sort of buffer between the princes of the empire and the imperial power, to which they often looked for protection against their immediate overlord or their powerful neighbour — the prince. The imperial power, in consequence, found the lower nobility a bulwark against its princely vassals. Economic changes, the suddenly increased demand for money owing to the rise of the "world-market," new inventions in the art of war, new methods of fighting, the rapidly growing importance of artillery and the increase of the mercenary soldiery, had rendered the lower nobility, as an institution, a factor in the political situation which was fast becoming negligible. The abortive campaign of Franz von Sickingen in 1523 only showed its hopeless weakness. The "Reichsregiment," or imperial governing council, a body instituted by Maximilian, had lamentably failed to effect anything; towards cementing together the various parts of the unwieldy fabric. Finally, at the "Reichstag" held in Nürnberg, in December, 1522, at which all the estates were represented, the "Reichsregiment," to all intents and purposes, collapsed.

The Reichstag in question was summoned ostensibly for the purpose of raising a subsidy for the Hungarians in their struggle against the advancing power of the Turks. The Turkish movement westward was, of course, throughout this period, the most important question of what in modern phraseology would be called "foreign politics". The princes voted the proposal of the subsidy without consulting the representatives of the cities, who knew the heaviest part of the burden was to fall upon themselves. The urgency of the situation, however, weighed with them, with the result that they submitted after considerable remonstrance. The princes, in conjunction with their rivals, the lower nobility, next proceeded to attack the commercial monopolies, the first fruits of the rising capitalism, the appanage mainly of the trading companies and the merchant-magnates of the towns. This was too much for civic patience. The city representatives, who of course belonged to the civic aristocracy, waxed indignant. The feudal orders went on to claim the right to set up vexations tariffs in their respective territories whereby to hinder artificially the free development of the new commercial capitalist. This filled up the cup of endurance of the magnates of the cities. The city representatives refused their consent to the Turkish subsidy and withdrew. The next step was the sending of a deputation to the young Emperor Karl, who was in Spain, and whose sanction to the decrees of the Reichstag was necessary before their promulgation. The result of the conference held on this occasion was a decision to undermine the " Reichsregiment," and weaken the power of the princes, by whom and by whose tools it was manned, as a factor in the imperial constitution. As for the princes, while some of their number were positively opposed to it, others cared little one way or the other. Their chief aim was to strengthen and consolidate their power within the limits of their own territories, and a weak empire was perhaps better adapted for effecting this purpose than a stronger one, even though certain of their own order had a controlling voice in its administration. As already hinted, the collapse of the rebellious knighthood under Sickingen, a few weeks later, clearly showed the political drift of the situation in the haute politique of the empire.

The rising capitalists of the cities, the monopolists, merchant princes and syndicates, are the theme of universal invective throughout this period. To them the rapid and enormous rise in prices during the early years of the sixteenth century, the scarcity of money consequent on the increased demand for it, and the impoverishment of large sections of the population, were attributed by noble and peasant alike. The whole trend of public opinion, in short, outside the wealthier burghers of the larger cities — the class immediately interested — was adverse to the condition of things created by the new world-market, and by the new class embodying it. At present it was a small class, the only one that gained by it, and that gained at the expense of all the other classes.

Some idea of the class-antagonisms of the period may be gathered from the statement of Ulrich von Hutten, in his dialogue entitled "Predones," that there were four orders of robbers in Germany — the knights, the lawyers, the priests, and the merchants (meaning especially the new capitalist merchant-traders or syndicates). Of these, he declares the robber-knights to be the least harmful. This is naturally only to be expected from so gallant a champion of his order, the friend and abettor of Sickingen. Nevertheless, the seriousness of the robber-knight evil, the toleration of which in principle was so deeply ingrained in the public opinion of large sections of the population, may be judged from the abortive attempts made to stop it, at the instance alike of princes and of cities, who on this point, if on no other, had a common interest. In 1502, for example, at the Reichstag held in Gelnhausen in that year, certain of the highest princes of the empire made a representation that, at least, the knights should permit the gathering in of the harvest and the vintage in peace. But even this modest demand was found to be impracticable. The knights had to live in the style required by their status, as they declared, and where other means were more and more failing them, their ancient right or privilege of plunder was indispensable to Hutten was right so far in declaring the knight the most harmless kind of robber, inasmuch as, direct as were his methods, his sun was obviously setting, while as much could not be said of the other classes named; the merchant and the lawyer were on the rise, and the priest, although about to receive a check, was not destined to speedily disappear, or to change fundamentally the character of his activity.

The feudal orders saw their own position seriously threatened by the new development of things economic in the; cities. The guilds were becoming crystallised into close corporations of wealthy families, constituting a kind of second Ehrbarkeit or town patriciate; the numbers of the landless and unprivileged, with at most a bare footing in the town constitution, were increasing in an alarming proportion; the journeyman-workman was no longer a stage between apprentice and master-craftsman, but a permanent condition embodied in a large and growing class. All these symptoms indicated an extraordinary economic revolution, which was making itself at first directly felt only in the larger cities, but the results of which were dislocating the social relations of the Middle Ages throughout the whole empire.

Perhaps the most striking feature in this dislocation was the transition from direct barter to exchange through the medium of money, and the consequent suddenly increased importance of the role played by usury in the social life of the time. The scarcity of money is a perennial theme of complaint for which the new large capitalist-monopolists are made responsible. The class in question was itself only a symptom of the general economic change. The seeming scarcity of money, though but the consequence of the increased demand for a circulating medium, was explained to the disadvantage of the hated monopolists by a crude form of the "mercantile" theory. The new merchant, in contradistinction to the master-craftsman working en famille with his apprentices and assistants, now often stood entirely outside the processes of production as speculator or middleman; and he, and still more the syndicate who fled the like functions on a larger scale (especially with reference to foreign trade), came be regarded as particularly obnoxious robbers, because interlopers to boot. Unlike the knights, they were robbers with a new face.

The lawyers were detested for much the same reason (cf. German Society at the Close of the Middle Ages, pp.219-228), the professional lawyer-class, since its final differentiation from the clerk-class in general, had made the Roman or civil law its speciality, and had done its utmost everywhere to establish the principles of the latter in place of the old feudal law of earlier mediaeval Europe. The Roman law was especially favourable to the pretensions of the princes, and, from an economic point of view, of the nobility in general, inasmuch as land was on the new legal principles treated as the private property of the lord, over which he had full power of ownership, and not, as under feudal and canon law, as a trust involving duties as well as rights. The class of jurists was itself of comparatively recent growth in Central Europe, and its rapid increase in every portion of the empire dated from less than half a century back. It may be well understood, therefore, why these interlopers, who ignored the ancient customary law of the country, and who by means of an alien code deprived the poor freeholder or copyholder of his land, or justified new and unheard-of exactions on the part of his lord on the plea that the latter might do what he liked with his own, were regarded by the peasant and humble man as robbers whose depredations were, if anything, even more resented than those of their old and tried enemy — the plundering knight.

The priest, especially of the regular orders, was indeed an old foe, but his offence had now become very rank. From the middle of the fifteenth century onwards the stream of anti-clerical literature waxes alike in volume and intensity. The "monk" had become the object of hatred and scorn throughout the whole lay world. This view of the "regular" was shared, moreover, by not a few of the secular clergy themselves. Humanists, who were subsequently ardent champions of the Church against Luther and the Protestant Reformation — men such as Murner and Erasmus had been previously bitterest satirists of the "friar" and the "monk". Amongst the great body of the laity, however, though the religious orders came perhaps for the greater share of animosity, the secular priesthood was not much better off in popular favour, whilst the upper members of hierarchy were naturally regarded as the chief blood-suckers of the German people in the interests of Rome. The vast revenues which both directly in the shape of pallium, the price of "investiture"), annates (first year's revenues of appointments, Peter's Pence, and recently of indulgences — the latter the by no means most onerous exaction, since it was voluntary, though proving as it happened the proverbial "last straw " — all these things, taken together with what was indirectly obtained from Germany, through the expenditure of German 'ecclesiastics on their visits to Rome and by the crowd of parasites, nominal holders of German benefices merely, but real recipients of German substance, who danced attendance at the Vatican — obviously constituted an enormous drain on the resources of the country from all the lay classes alike, of which wealth the papal chair could be plainly seen to be the receptacle.

If we add to these causes of discontent the vastness in number of the regular clergy, the "friars" and "monks" already referred to, who consumed, but were only too obviously unproductive, it will be sufficiently plain that the Protestant Reformation had something very much more than a purely speculative basis to work upon. Religious reformers there had been in Germany throughout the Middle Ages, but their preachings had taken no deep root. The powerful personality of the Monk of Wittenberg found an economic soil ready to hand in which his teachings could fructify, and hence the world-historic result. As we saw in the former volume of this history, the peasant revolts, sporadic the Middle Ages through, had for the half-century preceding the Reformation been growing in frequency and importance, but it needed nevertheless the sudden impulse, the powerful jar given by a Luther in 1517, the series of blows with which it was followed during the years immediately succeeding, to crystallise the mass of fluid discontent and social unrest in its various forms and give it definite direction. The blow which was primarily struck in the region of speculative thought and ecclesiastical relations did not stop there in its effects. The attach on the dominant theological system — at first merely on certain comparatively unessential outworks of system — necessarily of its own force developed into an attack on the organisation representing it, and on the economic basis of the latter. The battle against ecclesiastical abuses, again, in its turn, focussed the ever-smouldering discontent with abuses in general; and this time, not in one district only, but simultaneously over the whole of Germany. The movement inaugurated by Luther gave to the peasant groaning under the weight of baronial oppression, and the small handicraftsman suffering under his Eharbarkeit, a rallying point and a rallying cry.

In history there is no movement which starts up full grown from the brain of any one man, or even from the mind of any one generation of men, like Athene from the head of Zeus. The historical epoch which marks the crisis of the given change is after all little beyond a prominent landmark — parting of the ways — led up to by a long preparatory development. This is nowhere more clearly illustrated than in the Reformation and its accompanying movements. The ideas and aspirations animating the social, political and intellectual revolt of the sixteenth century can each be traced back to, at least, the beginning of the fifteenth century, and in many cases farther still. The way the German of Luther's time looked at the burning questions of the hour was not essentially different from the way the English Wycliffites and Lollards or the Bohemian Hussites and Taborites viewed them. There was obviously a difference born of the later time, but this difference was not, I repeat essential. The changes which, a century previously, were only just be beginning, had, meanwhile, made enormous progress. The disintegration of the material conditions of mediaeval social life was now approaching its completion, forced on by the inventions and discoveries of the previous half-century. But the ideals of the mass of men, learned and simple, were still in the main the ideals that had been prevalent throughout the whole of the later Middle Ages. Men still looked at the world and at social progress through mediaeval spectacles. The chief difference was that now ideas which had previously been confined to special localities, or had only had a sporadic existence among the people at large, had become general throughout large portions of the population. The invention of the art of printing was of course largely instrumental in effecting this change.

The comparatively sudden popularisation of doctrines previously confined to special circles was the distinguishing feature of the intellectual life of the first half of the sixteenth century. Among the many illustrations of the foregoing which might be given, we are specially concerned here to note the sudden popularity during this period of two imaginary constitutions dating from early in the previous century. From the fourteenth century we find traces, perhaps suggested by the Prester John legend, of a deliverer in the shape of an emperor who should come from the East, who should be the last of his name; should right all wrongs; should establish the empire in universal justice and peace; and, in short, should be the forerunner of the kingdom of Christ on earth. This notion or mystical hope took increasing root during the fifteenth century, and is to be found in many respects embodied in the spurious constitutions mentioned, which bore respectively the names of the Emperors Sigismund and Friedrich. It was in this form that the

Hussite theories were absorbed by the German mind. First of all, it was the eccentric and romantic Emperor Friedrich II. who was conceived of as playing the rôle in question. Later, the hopes of the Messianists of the "Holy Rooman Empire" were centred in the Emperor Sigismund. Later on still the rôle of the former Friedrich was carried over to his successor, Friedrich III., upon whom the hopes of the German people were cast.

The Reformation of Kaiser Sigismund, originally written about 1438, went through several editions before the end of the century, and was many times reprinted during the opening years of Luther's movement. Like its successor, that of Friedrich, the scheme attributed to Sigmund proposed the abolition of the recent abuses of feudalism, of the new lawyer class, and of the symptoms already making themselves felt of the change from barter to money payments. It proposed, in short a return to primitive conditions. It was a scheme of reform on a Biblical basis, embracing many elements of a distinctly communistic character, as communism was then understood. It was pervaded with the idea of equality in spirit of the Taborite literature of the age, from which it dated its origin. The so-called Reformation of Kaiser Sigismund dealt especially with the peasantry — the serfs and villeins of the time; that attributed to Friedrich was mainly concerned with the rising population of the towns. All towns and communes were to undergo a constitutional transformation. Handicraftsmen should receive just wages; all roads should be free; taxes, dues and levies should be abolished; trading capital was to be limited to a maximum of 10,000 gulden; all surplus capital should fall to the imperial authorities, who should lend it in case of need to poor handicraftsmen at five per cent.; uniformity of coinage and of weights and measures was to be decreed, together with the abolition of the Roman and Canon law. Legists, priests and princes were to be severely dealt with. But, curiously enough, the middle and lower nobility, especially the knighthood, were more tenderly handled, being treated as themselves victims of their feudal superiors, lay and ecclesiastic, especially the latter. In this connection the secularisation of ecclesiastical fiefs was strongly insisted on.

As men found, however, that neither the Emperor Sigismund, nor the Emperor Friedrich III., nor the Emperor Maximilian, upon each of whom successively their hopes had been cast as the possible realisation of the German Messiah of earlier dreams, fulfilled their expectations, nay, as each in succession implicitly belied these hopes, showing no disposition whatever to act up to the views promulgated in their names, the tradition of the imperial deliverer gradually lost its force and popularity. By the opening of the Lutheran Reformation the opinion had become general that change would not come from above, but that the initiative must rest with the people themselves — with the classes specially oppressed by existing conditions, political, economic and ecclesiastical — to effect by their own exertions such a transformation as was shadowed forth in the spurious constitutions. These, and similar ideas, were now everywhere taken up and elaborated, often in a still more radical sense than the original; and they everywhere found hearers and adherents.

The "true inwardness" of the change, of which the Protestant Reformation represented the ideological side, meant the transformation of society from a basis mainly corporative and co-operative to one individualistic in its essential character. The whole polity of the middle ages, industrial, social, political, ecclesiastical, and based on the principle of the group or the community — ranging in hierarchical order from trade-guild to the town corporation; from the town corporation through the feudal orders to the imperial throne itself; from the single monastery to the order as a whole; and from the order as a whole to the complete hierarchy of the Church as represented by the papal chair. The principle of this social organisation was now breaking down. The modern and bourgeois conception of the autonomy of the individual in all spheres of life was beginning to affirm itself.

The most definite expression of this new principle asserted itself in the religious sphere. Individualism which was inherent in early Christianity, but which was present as a speculative content merely, had not been strong enough to counteract even the remains of corporate tendencies on the material side of things, in the decadent Roman Empire; and infinitely less so the vigorous group-organisation and sentiment of the northern nations, with their tribal society and communistic traditions still mainly intact. And these were the elements out of which mediaeval society arose. Naturally enough the new religious tendencies in revolt against the mediaeval corporate Christianity of the Catholic Church seized upon this individualistic element in Christianity, declaring the chief end of religion to be a personal salvation, for the attainment of which the individual himself was sufficing, apart from Church organisation and Church tradition. This served as a valuable destructive weapon for the iconoclasts in their attack on ecclesiastical privilege; consequently, in religion, this doctrine of Individualism rapidly made headway. But in more material matters the old corporative instinct was still too strong and the conditions were as yet too imperfectly ripe for the speedy triumph of Individualism.

The conflict of the two tendencies is curiously exhibited in the popular movements of the Reformation time. As enemies of the decaying and obstructive forms of Feudalism and Church organisation, the peasant and handicraftsman were necessarily on the side of the new Individualism. So far as negation and destruction were concerned, they were working apparently for the new order of things that new order of things which longo intervallo has finally landed in the developed capitalistic Individualism of nineteenth century. Yet when we come to consider their constructive programmes we find the positive demands put forward are based either on ideal conceptions derived from reminiscences of primitive communism, or else that they distinctly postulate a return to a state of things — the old mark organisation — upon which the later feudalism had in various ways encroached, and finally superseded. Hence, they were, in these respects, not merely not in the trend of contemporary progress, but in actual opposition to it; and therefore, as Lasalle justly remarked, they were necessarily and any case doomed to failure in the long run. This point should not be lost sight of in considering the various popular movements of the earlier half of the sixteenth century. The world was still essentially mediaeval; men were still dominated by mediaeval ways of looking at things and still immersed in medieval conditions of life. It is true that out of this mediaeval soil the new individualistic society was beginning to grow, but its manifestations were as yet not so universally apparent as to force a recognition of their real meaning. It was still possible to regard the various symptoms of change, numerous as they were, and far-reaching as we now see them to have been, as sporadic phenomena, as rank but unessential overgrowths on the old society, which it was possible by pruning and the application of other suitable remedies to get rid of, and thereby to restore a state of pristine health in the body political and social.

Biblical phrases and the notion of Divine justice now took the place in the popular mind formerly occupied by Church and Emperor. All the then oppressed classes of society — the small peasant, half villein, half free-man; the landless journeyman and town-proletarian; the beggar by the wayside; the small master, crushed by usury or tyrannised over by his wealthier colleague in the guild, or by the town-patriciate; even the impoverished knight, or the soldier of fortune defrauded of his pay; in short, all with whom times were bad, found consolation for their wants and troubles, and at the same time an incentive to action, in the notion of a Divine Justice which should restore all things, and the advent of which was approaching. All had Biblical phrases tending in the direction of their immediate aspirations in their mouths. As bearing on the development and propaganda of the new ideas, the existence of a new intellectual class, rendered possible by the new method of exchange through money (as opposed that of barter), which for a generation past had been in full swing in the larger towns, had not been forgotten. Formerly land had been the essential condition of livelihood; now it was no longer so. The "universal equivalent," money, conjoined with the printing press, was rendering a literary class proper, for the first time possible. In the same way the teacher, e small lawyer were enabled to subsist as followers of independent professions, apart from the special service of the Church or as part of the court-retinue of some feudal potentate. To these we must add a fresh and very important section of the intellectual class which also now for the first time acquired an independent existence — to wit, that of the public official or functionary. This change, although only one of many, is itself specially striking as indicating the transition from the barbaric civilisation of the Middle Ages to the beginnings of the civilisation of the Modern World. We have, in short, before us, as already remarked, a period in which the Middle Ages, whilst still dominant, have their force visibly sapped by the growth of a new life.

To sum up the chief features of this new life: Industrially, we have the decline of the old system of production in the countryside in which each manor or, at least, each district, was for the most part self-sufficing and self-supporting, where production was almost entirely for immediate use, and only the surplus was exchanged, arid where such exchange as existed took place exclusively under the form of barter. In place of this, we find now something more than the beginnings of a national-market and distinct traces of that of a world-market. In the towns the change was even still more marked. Here we have a sudden and hothouse-like development of the influence of money. The guild system, originally designed for associations of craftsmen, for which the chief object was the man and the work, and not the mere requirement of profit, was changing its character. The guilds were becoming close corporations of privileged capitalists, while a commercial capitalism, as already indicated, was raising its head in all the larger centres. In consequence of this state of things, the rapid development of the towns and of commerce, national and international, and the economic backwardness of the countryside, a landless proletariat was being formed, which meant on the one hand an enormous increase in mendicancy of all kinds, and on the other the creation of a permanent class of only casually-employed persons, whom towns absorbed indeed, but for the most part with a new form of citizenship involving only the bare right of residence within the walls. Similar social phenomena were of course manifesting themselves contemporaneously in other parts of Europe; but in Germany the change was more sudden than elsewhere, and was complicated by special political circumstances.

The political and military functions of that for the mediaeval polity of Germany, so important class, the knighthood, or lower nobility, had by this time become practically obsolete, mainly owing to the changed conditions of warfare. But yet the class itself was numerous, and still, nominally at least, possessed of most of its old privileges and authority. The extent of its real power depended, however, upon the absence or weakness of a central power, whether imperial or state-territorial. The attempt to reconstitute the centralised power of the empire under Maximilian, of which the Reichsregiment was the outcome, had, as we have seen, not proved successful. Its means of carrying into effect its own decisions were hopelessly inadequate. In 1523 it was already weakened, and became little more than a "survival" after the Reichstag held at Nürnburg in 1524. Thus this body, which had been called into existence at the instance of the most powerful estates of the empire, was "shelved" with the practically unanimous consent of those who had been instrumental in creating it. But if the attempt at imperial centralisation had failed, the force of circumstances tended partly for this very reason to favour state-territorial centralisation. The aim of all the territorial magnates, the higher members of the imperial system, was to consolidate their own princely power within the territories owing them allegiance. This desire played a not unimportant part in the establishment of the Reformation in certain parts of the country — for example, in Würtemberg, and in the northern lands of East Prussia which were subject to the Grand Master of the Teutonic knights. The time was at hand for the transformation of the medieval feudal territory, with its local jurisdictions and its ties of service, into the modern bureaucratic state, with its centralised administration and organised system of salaried functionaries subject to a central authority.

The religious movement inaugurated by Luther met and was absorbed by all these elements of change. It furnished them with a religious flag, order cover of which they could work themselves out. This was necessary in an age when the Christian theology was unquestioningly accepted in one or another form by well-nigh all men, and hence entered as a practical belief into their daily thoughts and lives. The Lutheran Reformation, from its inception m 1517 down to the Peasants War of 1525, at once absorbed, and was absorbed by, all the revolutionary elements of the time. Up to the last-mentioned date it gathered revolutionary force year by year. But this was the turning point. With the crushing of the peasants' revolt and the decisively anti-popular attitude taken up by Luther, the religious movement associated with him ceased any longer to have a revolutionary character. It henceforth became definitely subservient to the new interests of the wealthy and privileged classes, and as such completely severed itself from the more extreme popular reforming sects. Up to this time, though by no means always approved by Luther himself or his immediate followers, and in some cases even combated by them, the latter were nevertheless not looked upon with disfavour by large numbers of the rank and the of those who regarded Martin Luther as their leader. Nothing could exceed the violence of language with which Luther himself attacked all who stood in his way. Not only the ecclesiastical, but also the secular heads of Christendom came in for the coarsest abuse; "swine" "water-bladder" are not the strongest epithets employed. But this was not all; in his Treatise on Temporal Authority and how far it should be Obeyed published in 1523), whilst professedly maintaining the thesis that the secular authority is a Divine ordinance, Luther none the less expressly justifies resistance to all human authority where its mandates are contrary to "the word of God". At the same time, he denounces in his customary energetic language the existing powers generally. Thou shouldst know," he says "that since the beginning of the world a wise prince is truly a rare bird, but a pious prince is still more rare. They (prince's) are mostly the greatest fools or the greatest rogues on earth; therefore must we at all times expect from them the worst, and little good." Farther on, he proceeds: "The common man begetteth understanding, and the plague of the princes worketh powerfully among the people and the common man. He will not, he cannot, he purposeth not, longer to suffer your tyranny and oppression. Dear princes and lords, know ye what to do, for

God will no longer endure it? The world is no more as of old time, when ye hunted and drove the people as your quarry. But think ye to carry on with much drawing of sword, look to it that one do not come who shall bid ye sheath it, and that not in God's name!' again, in a pamphlet published the following year, 1524, relative to the Reichstag of that year, Luther proclaims that the judgment of God already awaits "the drunken and mad princes". He quotes the phrase: "Deposuit potentes de sede" (Luke i.52), and adds " that is your case, dear lords, even now, when ye see it not"! After an admonition to subjects to refuse to go forth to war against the Turks, or to pay taxes towards resisting them, who were ten times wiser and more godly than German princes, the pamphlet concludes with the prayer "May God deliver us from ye all, and of His grace give us other rulers"! Against such utterances as the above, the conventional exhortations to Christian humility, non-resistance, and obedience to those in authority, would naturally not weigh in a time of popular ferment. So, until the momentous year 1525, it was not unnatural that, notwithstanding his quarrel with Münzer and the Zwickau enthusiasts, and with others whom he deemed to be going "too far," Luther should have been regarded as in some sort the central figure of the revolutionary movement, political and social, no less than religious.

But the great literary and agitator forces during the period referred to were of course either outside the Lutheran movement proper or at most only on the fringe of it. A mass of broadsheets and pamphlets, specimens of some of which have been given in a former volume (German Society at the Close of the Middle Ages, pp. 114-128), poured from the press during these years, all with the refrain that things had gone on long enough, that the common man, be he peasant or townsman, could no longer bear it. But even more than the revolutionary literature were the wandering preachers effective m working up the agitation which culminated in the Peasarts War of 1525. The latter comprised men of all classes, from the impoverished knight, the poor priest, the escaped monk, or the travelling scholar, to the peasant, the mercenary soldier out of employment, the poor handicraftsman, or even the beggar. Learned and simple, they wandered about from place to place, in the market place of the town, in the common field of the village, from one territory to another, preaching the gospel of discontent. Their harangues were, as a rule, as much political as religious, and the ground tone of them all was the social or economic misery of the time, and the urgency of immediate action to bring about a change. As in the literature, so in the discourses, Biblical phrases designed to give force to the new teaching abounded. The more thorough-going of these itinerant apostles openly aimed at nothing less than the establishment of a new Christian Commonwealth, or, as they termed it, "the Kingdom of God on Earth".

This vast agitation throughout Central Europe reached its climax in 1524, in the autumn and winter of which year definite preparations were in many places made for the general rebellion which was to break out in the following spring.

In describing the course of the movement known as the Peasants War, since there is no concerted campaign throughout the whole of the districts affected, to be recorded, it is impossible to preserve complete chronological order. The several outbreaks, though the result of a common agitation working upon a common discontent, engendered by conditions everywhere essentially the same, had each of them its own local history and its own local colour. There was no general preconcerted plan of campaign, and this, as we shall see, was the main cause of the comparatively speedy and signally disastrous collapse of the movement. The outbreaks occurred for the most part simultaneously or within a few days of each other, but the immediate cause was often some local circumstance, and no sufficient communication was kept up, even between districts where this would not have been difficult, while any concerted action between the peasant forces of north and central, or of central and southern Germany, was scarcely even thought of

Like all other movements of the time, that of the peasants and small townsmen had a strong infusion of religious sentiment based Christian theology. It was, it is true, primarily an economic and social agitation, but it had a strong religious colouring. The invocation of Christian doctrine and Biblical sentiments was no mere external flourish, but formed part of the essence of the movement. It must also be remembered that there was more than one side to the agitation; for example, the of Thomas Münzer, whose name most prominently associated with he social revolution of 1525, was confined to one town, and it is doubtful whether it was really accepted by all the insurrectionary elements, even in Mühlhausen, not to speak of the rest of Thuringia. There was undoubtedly a sub-conscious communistic element underlying the whole uprising, but for the most part it was little more than a sentiment which took no definite shape. While partially successful in impressing his teaching on the Thuringian revolt, Münzer it seems had little success in Franconia or in southern Germany. Indeed, the south Germans appear to have been actually averse to any definite utopistic idealism such as that of Thomas Münzer, and to have tended to confine themselves strictly to the limits of the celebrated "twelve articles". It is, moreover, in the latter document, which certainly comes from a south German source, that we find formulated the definite demands which constituted the practical basis of the movement generally. In the "twelve articles" we have expressed undoubtedly the ideas and aspirations of the average man throughout Germany who took part in the movement. What went beyond these demands was mere vague sentiment, in which possibly the average man shared but which did not take definite shape in his mind. In this remarkable document, the precise authorship of which is matter of conjecture only, we have unquestionably the best expression of the average public opinion of the "peasant" of Central Europe in the first half of the sixteenth century.

Notes

1. German Society at the Close of the Middle Ages, by E. Belfort Bax (Swan Sonnenschein & co., London, 1891).

2. It should he remembered that Germany at this time was cut up into feudal territorial divisions of all sizes, from the principality, or the prince-bishopric, to the knightly manor. Every few miles, and sometimes less, there was a fresh territory, a fresh lord, and a fresh jurisdiction.

Chapter II. The Outbreak of the Peasants War

THE growing discontent among the peasantry had led to many an attempt to curtail the right of assembly in the rural districts throughout Germany. These attempts were specially aimed at the popular merry-makings and festivals which brought the inhabitants of. Different parishes together. Weddings, pilgrimages, church-ales (kirchweihen), guild-feasts, etc., were sought to be suppressed or curtailed in many places. Even the ancient right of the village assembly was entrenched upon, or, in some cases, altogether withdrawn. But it was all of no avail. The fermentation continued to grow. From the spring of 1524 onwards, sporadic disturbances took place on various manors throughout the country. In many places tithes(1) were refused.

The first serious outbreak occurred in August, 1524, in the Rhine valley, in the Black Forest, at Stühlingen, on the domains of the Count of Lupfen, and the immediate cause is said to have been trivial exactions on the part of the countess. She required her tenants on some church holiday to gather strawberries and to collect snail shells on which to wind her skeins after spinning.(2) This slight impost evoked a spark that speedily became a flame running through all the neighbouring manors, where the various forms of corvée and dues were simultaneously refused. A leader suddenly appeared in one Hans Müller, a former soldier of fortune, who was a native of the village of Bulgenbach, belonging to the monastery of St. Blasien. A flag of the imperial colours, black, red and yellow, was made, and on St. Bartholomew's Day, the 24th August, Hans Müller at the head of 1,200 peasants marched to Waldshut under cover of a church-ale which was being held in that town.

Waldshut, which constituted the most eastern of the four so-called "forest towns" — the others being Laufenburg, Säkingen and Rheinfelden — was, at this moment, in strained relations with the Austrian authorities.

The peasants fraternised with the inhabitants of the little town, and the first "Evangelical Brotherhood" sprang into existence.(3) Every member of this organisation was required to contribute a small coin weekly to defray the expenses of the bearers of the secret despatches, which were to be distributed far and wide throughout Germany, inciting to amalgamation and a general rising. Throughout the districts of Baden in the Black Forest, throughout Elsass, the Rhein, the Mosel territories, as far as Thuringia, the message ran: no lord should there be but the emperor, to whom proper tribute should be rendered, on the guarantee of their ancient rights, but all castles and monasteries should be destroyed together with their charters and their jurisdictions.

As soon as the news of the agitation reached the Swabian League, unsuccessful attempts at pacification were made. The Swabian League, it must be premised, was a federation of princes, barons and towns, whose function was keeping up an armed force for the main purpose of seeing that imperial decrees were carried out, and for preserving public tranquillity generally. It was really the only effective instrument of imperial power that existed. As we shall presently see, it was this Swabian League that chiefly contributed to crushing the peasant revolt throughout southern Germany. Meanwhile the forces of Hans Muller were growing, until by the middle of October well-nigh 5,000 men were ranged under the black, red and gold banner. At the same time, the troops at the disposal of the nobility within the revolting area were altogether inadequate to cope with the situation. In the districts of the Black Forest and elsewhere, the Italian War of Charles V. had drained off the best and most numerous of the fighting men.

After marching through the neighbouring districts with his peasant army, whose weapons consisted largely of pitchforks, scythes and axes, proclaiming the principles and the objects of the revolt, Hans Müller withdrew into a safe retreat in the neighbourhood of the village of Rietheim on learning that a small force of about a thousand men had been got together against him. The winter was now fast approaching, and it did not appear to the aristocratic party desirable for the time being to pursue matters any further in the direction of open hostilities.

Accordingly Hans von Friedingen, the Chancellor of the Bishop of Constanz, with three other gentlemen, proceeded to the camp of the peasants to attempt a negotiation. They succeeded in persuading the insurgents to disperse on the understanding that the lords specially inculpated should agree to consider proposals from their tenants, and that, failing an agreement on this basis, the matters in dispute should be referred to an independent tribunal, the district court of Stockach being suggested. A basis of agreement drawn up between the Count of Lupfen and his tenants contains some curious provisions; while fishing was prohibited, a pregnant woman having a strong desire for a fish was to be supplied with one by the bailiff. Bears and wolves were declared free game, but the heads were to be reserved for the lord, and in the case of bears one of the paws as well. Meanwhile, the towns of northern Switzerland, in whose territories an agitation was also proceeding, began to get alarmed and to warn the Black Forest bands off their territories. Switzerland herself was at this time in the throes of the Reformation, and in the neighbouring lands of the St. Gallen Monastery a vehement agitation was going on. No attempt, however, was made by the German peasants to pass over into Swiss territory, although it seems to have been more than once threatened. Zürich, Schaffhausen, and other Swiss cantons, indeed, in the earlier phases of the Peasants War, endeavoured to effect a mediation between the peasants and their lords. They were partly afraid of the agitation taking dangerous form with their own peasants and partly regarded the movement as belonging to the religious reformation, which had now taken root in northern Switzerland.

The following articles were agreed upon as the basis of negotiation by the united peasants of the Black Forest and the neighbouring lands of Southern Swabia, which were also now involved in the movement:-

1. The obligation to hunt or fish for the lord was to be abolished, and all game, likewise fishing, was to be declared free.

2. They should no longer be compelled to hang bells on their dogs' necks.

3. They should be free to carry weapons.

4. They should not be liable to punishment from huntsmen and forest rangers.

5. They should no longer carry dung for their lord.

6. They should have neither to mow, reap, hew wood, nor carry trusses of hay nor firewood for the uses of the castle.

7. They were to be free of the heavy market tolls and handicraft taxes.

8. No one should be cast into the lord's dungeon or otherwise imprisoned who could give guarantees for his appearance at the judicial bar.

9. They should no longer pay any tax, due, or charge whatsoever the right to which had not been judicially established.

10. No tithe of growing corn should be exacted, nor any agricultural corvée.

11. Neither man nor woman should be any longer punished for marrying without the permission of his or her lord.

12. The goods of suicides should no longer revert to the lord.

13. The lord should no longer inherit where relations of the deceased were living.

14. All bailiff rights should be abolished.

15. He who had wine in his house should be at liberty to serve it to whomsoever he pleased.

16. If a lord or his bailiff arrested any one on account of a transgression which he was unable to prove with good witnesses, the accused should be set at liberty.

Such were the very moderate demands put forward by the peasants of the Black Forest districts, of the Klettgau, of the Hegau, and of the other manors associated with them. But the object of the feudal lords, as appears from the documents(4) which have subsequently come to light, was not peace on the basis of a fair understanding, but simply to hoodwink their tenants with the pretence of negotiations, until such time as they should have got together sufficient men to crush the rising and compel them to unconditional submission. The Archduke Ferdinand writes expressly as regards Georger Truchsess, Count of Waldburg, the chief commander of the forces of the Swabian League at this time, that he should "amicably treat with the peasants till he had collected his military forces together". But it was not easy to obtain fighting men at this time. The struggle between the Emperor and Francis I., which was being fought out in Italy, was reaching its most critical stage, and nobles and soldiers of fortune alike were being drafted off south. By the end of 1524 Germany was almost denuded of the usual supply of men-at-arms at the disposal of constituted authority, and there seemed no immediate prospect of their returning.

Meanwhile, the movement in the country districts and the small towns was growing and spreading on all sides. The leader of the Black Forest peasants, Hans Müller of Bulgenbach, in his red hat and mantle, was everywhere active. He succeeded in collecting together another force of some 6,000 men under his flag, most of whom, however, shortly afterwards dispersed, leaving him with only a small residue of their number and some free-lances. The latter attacked and destroyed the castle of the Count of Lupfen, where the outbreak in August had originated. Other bands formed also in neighbouring territories. Truchsess, the generalissimo of the Swabian League, was not inactive. With the comparatively small force he had collected, he kept the peasants under observation, alternately negotiating with and threatening them. But as winter was near, comparatively little was done on either side. The peasant bands sacked a few monasteries; and the Austrian authorities at Ensisheim, between Colmar and Mühlhausen in Elsass — the official seat of the hereditary Hapsburg power in the west — succeeded in gathering a small force, with which they attacked a body of the insurgents, burning some homesteads and seizing cattle. The day originally fixed for the opening of the arbitration between the lords and their tenants was the day of St. John the Evangelist, the 27th of December. When, however, the peasant delegates found that the court was composed entirely of noblemen, they entered a protest, and the proceedings had to be adjourned until 6th January, 1525 ("Three Kings' Day"). But the matter continued to grow more serious for the nobility, many of whom withdrew from their castles to Radolfzell and to other towns whose loyalty and means of defence offered sufficient guarantees of personal security. As many as three hundred clergy, some of them disguised as Landsknechte, and most of them with the tonsure covered, fled to Ueberlingen, on the Lake of Constanz.

The 6th of January came, and with it the delegations, not only of the peasants, but also, as had been agreed upon, of various towns lying within the disaffected districts; but neither the lords nor the representative of the Bishop of Constanz, appeared; consequently no court could be held, and matters remained in statu quo. Finally, on the 20th of January, what seems to have been a kind of informal meeting took place between Truchsess and some other representatives of the Austrian power on the one side and delegates from a section of the disaffected population on the other. Truchsess, by fair words and promises, succeeded in inducing a portion of those present to capitulate, but with the rest, notably with the inhabitants of the district called the Hegau, neither his promises nor his threats availed to make them consent to lay down their arms and disperse. They insisted upon their sixteen Articles, of which they refused to abate a single one. But the ruling classes now saw some prospect of acquiring an army sufficient to quell the threatened insurrection. The archduke had negotiated a loan from the Welsers of Augsburg, by means of which he was enabled to scour the country in the search for men-at-arms who might be willing to join the League's forces under Truchsess. This was now being done with partial success, and there seemed a prospect of the League being able to take the field against the insurgent populations, if necessary, within a few weeks. On the 15th of February, Truchsess sent the Hegau bands an insolent and impossible ultimatum, with the threat to pursue them without mercy on their failing to accept his conditions. In a few days the whole neighbouring country was up in arms. But the instructions from Innsbruck, from the archduke, who after all was timid and did not know how to act, considerably impeded the operations of Truchsess.

An accidental circumstance at this time caused a diversion favourable to the threatening insurrection. Duke Ulrich of Würtemberg was a fugitive from his ancestral domains under the ban of the Empire. Compelled to leave Würtemberg in 1519, on the grounds of a family quarrel, which had been decided against him by the imperial authorities, he had in vain sought help from the Swiss Confederation to re-establish himself, and was now constrained to turn to the very peasants whom he had driven out of his territories on the suppression of the rising known as that of "the poor Conrad" in 1514 (cf. German Society, pp.75-77). As he himself expressed it, he was determined to come to his rights, "if not by the aid of the spur, by that of the shoe," by which was meant, of course, that on the failure of the negotiations he was making with the knights and nobles of various districts, extending even to Bohemia, he was prepared to enter into a league with the rebellious peasants. In fact, he now adopted the affectation of signing himself "Utz Bur" ("Utz the Peasant") — Utz being the short for Ulrich — instead of "Ulrich, Duke". He had now established himself in his stronghold of Hohentwiel in Würtemberg, on the frontier of Switzerland. Negotiations with the disaffected had certainly been carried on over a wide extent of territory; and the imperial chancellor was emphatic in accusing Ulrich of fomenting the disorders.

Würtemberg, whose inhabitants, for the most part, detested the house of Austria, and, in spite of exactions and oppression, retained a certain feudal-patriotic affection for their hereditary overlord, was favourably disposed to his return. The opportunity seemed now to have arrived for a successful invasion of his patrimonial territory. His negotiations with the peasant bands were not wholly successful, since he was largely mistrusted by them. However, an arrangement was come to with Hans Müller of Bulgenbach, who arrived with a body of Black Forest and Hegau peasants to his assistance. In addition, he had engaged a large number of mercenaries from the northern Swiss cantons and elsewhere, so that by the end of February he was enabled to start on his campaign with an army of some 6,000 foot and 200 horse, besides a few pieces of artillery. But the Swabian League was beforehand with Duke Ulrich. At the instance of its commander George Truchsess, Count von Helfenstein seized Stuttgart, leaving a garrison within the walls, while the duke was slowly advancing. Truchsess rightly saw that, as capital of the duchy, Stuttgart was the key of the situation. The fact was that Ulrich had allowed his men to carouse too long on the way at the little town of Sindelfingen. Had he proceeded on to Stuttgart at once without stopping, he would probably have succeeded in entering his capital before Helfenstein. As it was, all he could do was. to lay siege to the town. To make matters worse for him, the news of the issue of the battle of Pavia, which was fought on the 24th of February, arrived. The signal victory obtained by the imperial forces decided the struggle between Charles V. and Francis I., which had until then been hanging in the balance. All whose interests, from whatever cause, were contrary to that of the emperor, Ulrich amongst the number, had naturally placed their hopes on the French king. These were now, of course, shattered. What was of more immediate importance was that the Archduke Ferdinand, as representing the victorious house of Austria and imperial power, had just seized the opportunity of insisting that the Swiss cantons should immediately order the return of their men, who were serving with the duke, on pain of outlawry and confiscation of goods. The cantons at this juncture did not dare to refuse the demand, and accordingly the order was issued; the Swiss free-lances, whose pay was in arrears, on its announcement, accompanied, it is said, by Austrian gold, promptly deserted and hurried back to their fatherland. Ulrich with his remaining forces was unable to continue the siege; indeed, he was glad enough in his turn to hurry back to his stronghold — his Hohentwiel — as quickly as possible. The Würtemberg peasants had not risen to his aid with the enthusiasm he had anticipated. Little as they might care for the Austrian regency in Würtemberg, the memory of "the poor Conrad," and of their friends and relations who had been driven from house and home on the suppression of that movement eleven years before, was too recent for them to be especially eager to sacrifice themselves to reinstate the man primarily responsible for their troubles. Thus ended this attempt of Duke Ulrich to recover his territory by the aid of peasants and mercenaries. The whole episode from first to last occupied. little more than three weeks, but during this time it served to divert the attention of the Swabian League.

The Swabian peasants, as already mentioned, had begun to stir in the autumn of 1524, at about the same time as those of the Black Forest and the Lake of Constanz districts. In Swabia, the first overt signs of disaffection showed themselves in the lands of the abbey of Kempten, and the immediate occasion of them appears to have been the imprisonment and harsh treatment by the abbot of an old man, a tenant of the abbey, on the ground of a disrespectful expression he had let fall concerning him during the haymaking. The abbot's despotic government of the manor had everywhere incensed the peasantry. The prince prelate, after having promised to consider the grievances in conjunction with other high personages on a given day, appeared indeed. and listened to the complaints laid before him, but it was only to give a categorical refusal to make any concession whatever. The result of his action was that those immediately concerned decided to call an assembly representing all the subjects of the extensive abbey territory, to lay the matter before them, and to consider what further course should be taken. On the 21st of January, a numerous assembly met together accordingly at a given place on the bank of the little stream called the Luibas, to take counsel as to further action. The little town of Kempten was in a ferment, part of the burghers sympathising with the peasants and part with the abbey.

The meeting, at which in addition to representatives of the whole countryside, some members of the town council (Rath) attended, kept its proceedings within the bounds of the strictest moderation, repudiating any hostile intentions with regard to the foundation, and finally decided to lay the dispute before a competent tribunal, all present pledging themselves and their respective villages to contribute to the cost of carrying it through. Three days later, the representatives met in Kempten itself, and chose a committee of their number to take steps in the matter. This committee immediately drew up a formal protest against the wrongs suffered from the abbot, which was forwarded to the council of the Swabian League and to the emperor. In this document was expressed the readiness of the villeins of the abbey to furnish all dues and all service to which the prince-prelate could establish his right by charter. On the other hand, it energetically protested against new and unjustifiable exactions and arbitrary oppressions, and prayed that the case might be laid before the supreme court of the district. The league, meanwhile, undertook to prevent their lord, the abbot, from taking any hostile steps against them pending the decision. The latter, however, immediately answered this protest by a letter addressed to the Swabian League, in which he accused his subjects of having entered into a conspiracy against the foundation and demanded armed intervention in his favour. The Councillors of the League, who were sitting in permanence at the imperial town of Ulm, temporised, promising to consider the grievances of the peasantry, and, should it prove impossible to effect an informal compromise, to see that the matter was legally decided by a competent authority.

By this time, the whole country north and south of Ulm was in a state of nascent insurrection. From Kempten northwards to the latter city, ecclesiastical foundations pressed hard on one another. Their tenants were everywhere desperately angry. In the district known from its swampy character as the Ried, a blacksmith named Schmidt constituted himself leader of the rising. In all the village inns thereabouts bodies of peasants daily came together to take counsel. On the 9th of February, a camp of some 2000 peasants was formed at a place called Leipheim. Another contingent was started which soon rose to nearly 13,000 men. Armed bodies of peasants were now forming themselves into camps throughout Southern Germany. The insurgents were divided into three main bodies — those of the Ried, of the Lake of Constanz districts, and of the Black Forest. In the course of the month, these divisions amalgamated into the so-called "Christian brotherhood". The leaders of the movement assembled at the small town of Memmingen, where the "Peasants Parliament" was held at the beginning of March, where in all probability the celebrated "Twelve Articles" were drawn up, and where they were certainly adopted. Here also the most studied moderation was observed in the demands made and in the proceedings generally. The decisions arrived at this conference of Memmingen were sworn to by all the camps throughout the country. The restoration of ancient privileges, where these had been abrogated, was demanded, such as the ancient right to carry arms, together with that of free assembly.

On the same day on which the order of federation was adopted, the representatives at Memmingen addressed a formal letter to the Swabian League explaining that the action taken was in accordance with the Gospel and with Divine Justice. The Christian Brotherhood was to form the bond of organisation for the whole country. A president and four councillors were to be chosen from every camp or organised body of peasants. These should have plenary powers to enter into agreements with other similar camps or bodies, as well as in certain cases to negotiate with constituted authorities. No one was to enter into an agreement with his feudal lord without the consent of the whole countryside, and even where such consent was granted the tenants in question should nevertheless continue to belong to the Christian Brotherhood and to be subject to its decisions. Any who from any cause had to leave their native place should first swear before the headman of the district to do nothing to the hurt of the Christian Brotherhood, but to assist it by word and deed wherever necessary. The existing judicial functions should continue in exercise as before. Unbecoming pastimes, blasphemy and drunkenness should be forbidden, and all such offences duly punished. Lastly, no one should, from any cause whatever, undertake any action against his lord, or commit any trespass on his lands or goods, until a further decision had been taken. There was now, therefore, it will be seen, a definite organisation of the peasantry throughout the whole of the South German territories — an organisation prepared for action at any moment.

The Black Forest, the Duchy of Würtemberg, and Eastern or Upper Swabia were already organised. In the course of this month of March, the Episcopal territories of Bamberg, of Würtzburg, the Franconian districts generally, Bavaria, Tyrol, and the Arch-episcopal territories of Salzburg, rose — from Thuringia in the north to the Alpine lands in the south, from Elsass and Lorraine in the west to the Austrian hereditary dominions in the east, the whole of Central Europe was astir. The "common man" was everywhere in evidence. By the beginning of April, as though it had been concerted, the Peasants War had broken out throughout Germany.

Before giving a sketch of the chief incidents connected with the rising, we will cast a glance at the formulated demands represented in the "Twelve Articles," at the different currents embodied in the movement, and at the men who were its intellectual heads — Weigand, Hipler, Karlstadt, Gaismayr, Hubmayer, reserving Münzer and Pfeiffer for a subsequent chapter.

Notes

1. The tithe was of two kinds, the so-called great tithe and the little tithe. The great tithe consisted usually of crops (of hay, corn, barley, etc.); the little tithe generally of a head of cattle. This latter appears to have been especially obnoxious to the peasantry.

2. This story represents the uniform tradition; but although not refuted, it is not authenticated, by any contemporary documentary evidence.

3. This is the view taken by Zimmermann, the great historian of the Peasants War, but it should be mentioned that Bezold and other later authorities are of the opinion that no formal association of this kind was constituted on this occasion, although they admit that an informal fraternisation took place, which was not without its results on the ensuing agitation.

4. Cf. Archives of the Swabian League and the Weingarten Archives in the Schmidt collection, the substance of which is given in Zimmermann.

Chapter III. Demands, Ideals and Apostles of the Movement

ASTROLOGY and mystical prophesyings appeared in the times shortly preceding the great social upheaval, foretelling strange things which were to happen in the years 1524 and 1525.

One of the principal of these indicated a Noachic delude for the summer of 1524. This vaticination was based on an alleged combination of sixteen conjunctures in the sign of Aquarius. So seriously was the prophesy believed in that extensive preparations were made, in view of the approaching catastrophe. Many, however, explained the presage as indicating a social inundation — the levelling of social distinctions by the "common man". Portents were alleged to have appeared; strange monsters to have been born. Illustrated broadsheets and pamphlets were in circulation, on the title pages of which might be seen portrayed pope, emperor, cardinals and prince-prelates trembling before the approach of a band of peasants armed with the implements of husbandry and led on by the planet Saturn. All these things testified to the excited state of the public mind and the direction in which popular thought was turned. Meanwhile, the thinkers of the movement were preparing to give definite form to the vague aspirations of the multitude.

In the uprising known as the "Peasants War," as already stated, there is more than one strain to be observed, though all turns on the central ideas of equality, economic reform and political reorganisation. First of all, we have the immediate and practical side of the agrarian movement, on the lines of which the actual outbreak originated, and the special representatives of which were the peasants of South-Eastern Germany. This side of the movement is, of course, most prominently present everywhere, but in other parts of the country, notably in Franconia and Thuringia, it is accompanied by ideas of a more far-reaching kind as regards social reconstruction clothed in a mystical religious garb. Then again we have certain definite schemes of extensive political reform.

Behind these things lay the distinction between town and country, a distinction recently become so important. It need scarcely be said that most of those wider aspirations that entered into the movement had their origin in the new life of the towns, and, as regards their expression, in the more educated elements to be found within their walls. We will first cast a glance at the mainstay of the whole movement, the celebrated "Twelve Articles".

In the last chapter we have already seen a specimen of the immediate demands put forward by the peasants of the Black Forest. In these there is no mention of religion. They aptly indicate the position of the cultivator of the soil, robbed often of his common pasture, of the right of hunting and fishing on his own account; compelled to perform all sorts of services for his lord at any time, were it haymaking, harvest, or vintage, even though it meant to him the loss of his crop; made to furnish dues of every description payable in kind and now often in money; prohibited from catching, destroying, or driving away animals of the chase, even though they might be doing irreparable damage to agricultural produce; compelled to permit the lord's hunting dogs to devour his poultry at pleasure; Obliged to offer his live stock first of all to the castle before

selling it elsewhere; forced to furnish the castle with firewood and timber and (a significant item) wood for the stake, on the occasion of executions. And what was the penalty for the neglect of these things? Imprisonment in the lord's dungeon; the piercing out of eyes; or, in some cases, death itself. At first the remedying of such grievances was demanded in a different form on different manors, sometimes in a greater, sometimes in a lesser number of "Articles". Thus, in one case we find sixteen, in another thirty-four, in another sixty-two "points " in these several agrarian charters. In the month of March, 1525, however, they were all condensed into twelve main claims in a document entitled "The fundamental and just chief articles of all the peasantry and villeins of spiritual and temporal lordships by which they deem themselves opprest" This document was accepted practically throughout Germany as the basis of the revolution. Owing to its importance, we give this charter of the German peasantry in full. It reads as follows:-
INTRODUCTION.

"To the Christian reader, peace and the grace of God through Christ! There are many anti-Christians who now seek occasion to despise the Gospel on account of the assembled peasantry, in that they say: these be the fruits of the new Gospel: to obey none; to resist in all places; to bind together with great power of arms to the end to reform, to root out, ay and maybe to slay spiritual and temporal authority. All such godless and wicked judgments are answered in the articles here written down as well that they remove this shame from the Word of God as also that they may excuse in a Christian manner this disobedience, yea, this rebellion of all peasants.

"For the first time, the Gospel is not a cause of rebellion or uproar, since it is the word of Christ, the promised Messiah, whose word and life teaches naught save love, peace, patience and unity (Rom. xi.). Therefore, that all who believe in this Christ may be loving, peaceful, patient and united, such is the ground of all Articles of the peasants, and as may be clearly seen they are designed to the intent that men should have the Gospel and should live according thereto. How shall the anti-Christians then call the Gospel a cause of rebellion and of disobedience? But that certain anti-Christians and enemies of the Gospel should rise up against such requirements, of this is not the Gospel the cause, but the devil, the most hurtful enemy of the Gospel, who exciteth such by unbelief, in his own, that the Word of God which teacheth love, peace and unity may be trodden down and taken away.

"For the rest, it followeth clearly- and manifestly that the peasants who in their Articles require such Gospel as doctrine and as precept may not be called disobedient and rebellious. But should God hear those peasants who anxiously call upon Him that they may live according to his word; who shall gainsay the will of God? (Rom. xi.). Who shall Impeach His judgment? (Isa. xl.). Yea, who shall resist His Majesty? (Rom. viii.). Hath he heard the children of Israel and delivered them out of the hand of Pharoah, and shall He not to-day also save his own? Yea, He shall save them, and that speedily (Exod. iii 14; Luke xviii. 8). Therefore, Christian reader, read hereunder with care and thereafter judge.
FIRST ARTICLE

"For the first, it is our humble prayer and desire, also the will and opinion of us all that henceforth the power to choose and elect a pastor shall lie with the whole community (1 Tim. iii.),(1) that it shall also have the power to displace such an one, if he behaveth unseemly. The pastor that is chosen shall preach the Gospel plainly and manifestly, without any addition of man or the doctrine or ordinance of men (Acts xiv.). For that the true Faith is preached to us giveth us a cause to pray God for His grace that He implant within us the same living Faith and confirm us therein (Deut. xviii.; Exod. xxxi.). For if His grace be not implanted within us we remain flesh and blood which profiteth not (Deut. x.; John vi.). How plainly is it written in the Scripture that we can alone through the true Faith come to God and that alone through His mercy shall we be saved (Gal. i.). Therefore is such an ensample and pastor of need to us and in suchwise founded on the Scripture.

SECOND ARTICLE.

"Furthermore, notwithstanding that the just tithe was imposed in the Old Testament, and in the New was fulfilled, yet are we nothing loth to furnish the just tithe of corn, but only such as is meet, accordingly shall we give it to God and His servants (Heb.; also Ps. cix.). If it be the due of a pastor who clearly proclaimeth the Word of God, then it is our will that our church-overseers, such as are appointed by the community, shall collect and receive this tithe, and thereof shall give to the pastor who shall be chosen from a whole community suitable sufficient subsistence for him and his, as the whole community may deem just; and what remaineth over shall be furnished to the poor and the needy of the same village, according to the circumstance of the case and the judgment of the community (Deut. xxv.; 1 Tim. v.; Matt. x.; Cor. ix.). What further remaineth over shall be reserved for the event that the land being pressed, it should needs make war, and so that no general tax should be laid upon the poor, it shall be furnished from this surplusage. Should it be found that there were one or more villages that had sold the tithe itself because of need, he who can show respecting the same that he hath it in the form of a whole village shall not want for it but we will, as it beseemeth us, make an agreement with him, as the matter requireth (Luke vi.; Matt. v.) to the end that we may absolve the same in due manner and time. But to him who hath bought such from no village, and whose forefathers have usurped it for themselves, we will not, and we ought not to give him anything, and we owe no man further save as aforesaid that we maintain our elected pastors, that we absolve our just debts, or relieve the needy, as is ordained by the Holy Scripture. The small tithe will we not give, be it either to spiritual or to temporal lord; for the God the Lord bath created the beast freely for the use of man (Gen. i.). For we esteem this tithe for an unseemly tithe of man's devising. Therefore will we no longer give it.

THIRD ARTICLE.

"Thirdly, the custom hath hitherto been that we have been held for villeins; which is to be deplored, since Christ hath purchased and redeemed us all with His precious blood (Isa.lii; I Peter i.; I Cor. vii.; Rom. xiii.), the poor hind as well as the highest, none excepted. Therefore do we find in the Scripture that we are free; and we will be free (Eccles. vi.; I Peter ii.). Not that we would be wholly free as having no authority over us, for this God cloth not teach us. We shall live in obedience and not in the freedom of our fleshly pride (Deut. vi.; St. Matt. v.); shall love God as our Lord; shall esteem our neighbours as brothers; and do to them as we would have them do to us, as God hath commanded at the Last Supper (Luke iv. 6; Matt. v.; John xiii.). Therefore shall we live according to His ordinance. This ordinance in no wise sheweth us that we should not obey authority. Not alone should we humble ourselves before authority, but before every man (Rom. xiii.) as we also are gladly obedient in all just and Christian matters to such authority as is elected and set over us, so it be by God set over us (Acts v.). We are also in no doubt but that ye will as true and just Christians relieve us from villeinage, or will show us, out

of the Gospel, that we are villeins.
FOURTH ARTICLE.

"Fourthly, was it hitherto a custom that no poor man hath the right to capture ground game, fowls or fish in flowing water, which to us seemeth unbecoming and unbrotherly, churlish and not according to the Word of God. Moreover, in some places the authority letteth the game grow up to our despite and to our mighty undoing, since we must suffer that our own which God hath caused to grow for the use of man should be unavailingly devoured by beasts without reason, and that we should hold our peace concerning this, which is against God and our neighbours. For when God the Lord created man, he gave him power over all creatures, over the fowl in the air, and over the fish in the water (Gen. i.; Acts xix.; 1 Tim. iv.; Cor. x.; Coloss. xi.). Therefore it is our desire when one possess a water that he may prove it with sufficient writing as, unwittingly purchased. We do not desire to take such by force, but we must needs have a Christian understanding in the matter, because of brotherly love. But he who cannot bring sufficient proof thereof shall give it back to the community as beseemeth.
FIFTH ARTICLE.

"Fifthly, we are troubled concerning the woods; for our lords have taken unto themselves all the woods, and if the poor man requireth ought he must buy it with double money. Our opinion is as touching the woods, be they possessed by spiritual or temporal lords, whichsoever they be that have them and that have not purchased them, they shall fall again to the whole community, and that each one from out the community shall he free as is fitting to take therefrom into his house so much as he may need. Even for carpentering, if he require it, shall he take wood for nothing; yet with the knowledge of them who are chosen by the community to this end, whereby the destruction of the wood may be hindered; but where there is no wood but such as hath been honestly purchased, a brotherly and Christian agreement with the buyers shall be come to. But when one hath first of all taken to himself the land and hath afterwards sold it, then shall an agreement be entered into with the buyers according to the circumstance of the matter and with regard to brotherly love and Holy Writ.
SIXTH ARTICLE.

"Sixthly, our grievous complaint is as concerning the services which are heaped up from day to day and daily increased. We desire that these should be earnestly considered, and that we be not so heavily burdened withal; but that we, should be mercifully dealt with herein; that we may serve as our fathers have served and only according to the Word of God.
SEVENTH ARTICLE

"Seventhly, will we henceforth no longer be opprest by a lordship, but in such wise as a lordship. Hath granted the land, so shall it be held according to the agreement between the lord and the peasant. The lord shall no longer compel him and press him, nor require of him new services or aught else for naught (Luke iii.; Thess. vi.). Thus shall the peasant enjoy and use such land in peace, and undisturbed. But when the lord hath need of the peasant's services, the peasant shall be willing, and obedient to him before others; but it shall be at the hour and the time when it shall not be to the hurt of the peasant, who shall do his lord service for a befitting price.
EIGHTH ARTICLE

"Eighthly, there are many among us who are opprest in that they hold lands and in that these lands will not bear the price on them, so that the peasants must sacrifice that which belongeth to them, to their undoing. We desire that the lordship will let such lands be seen by honourable men, and will fix a price as may be just in such wise that the peasant may not have his labour in vain, for every labourer is worthy of his hire (Matt. x.).

NINTH ARTICLE.

"Ninthly, do we suffer greatly- concerning misdemeanours in that new punishments are laid upon us. They punish us not according to the circumstance of the matter, but sometimes from great envy, from the unrighteous favouring of others. We would be punished according to ancient written law, and according to the thing transgressed, and not according to respect of persons (Isa. x.; Eph. vi.; Luke iii.; Jer. xvi..

TENTH ARTICLE.

"Tenthly, we suffer in that some have taken to themselves meadows and arable land, which belong to a community. We will take the same once more into the hands of our communities wheresoever it hath not been honestly purchased. But hath it been purchased in an unjust manner, then shall the case be agreed upon in peace and brotherly love according to the circumstance of the matter.

ELEVENTH ARTICLE.

"Eleventhly, would we have the custom called the death-due utterly abolished, and will never suffer or permit that widows and orphans shall be shamefacedly robbed of their own, contrary to God and honour, as happeneth in many places and in divers manners. They have cut us short of what we possessed and should protect, and they have taken all. God will no longer suffer this, but it must be wholly ended. No man shall, henceforth, be compelled to give aught, be it little or much, as death-due (Deut. xiii.; Matt. viii.; Isa. x. 23).

TWELTH ARTICLE

"Twelfthly, it is our conclusion and final opinion, if one or more of the Articles here set up be not according to the word of God, we will, where the same articles are proved as against the Word of God, withdraw therefrom, so soon as this is declared to us by reason and Scripture; yea, even though certain Articles were now granted to us, and it should hereafter be found that they were unjust, they shall he deemed from that hour null and void and of none effect. The same shall happen if there should be with truth found in the Scripture yet more Articles which were against God and a stumbling-block to our neighbour, even though we should have determined to preserve such for ourselves, and we practice and use ourselves in all Christian doctrine, to which end we pray God the Lord who can vouchsafe us the same and none other. The peace of Christ be with us all."

Such are the celebrated "Twelve Articles". Such was the form in which they made the round of the countryside throughout Germany. They are moderate enough in all conscience, it must be admitted. It will be noticed that they embody the main demands of the Black Forest peasants, already quoted. The same may be said of other formulations of peasant requirements. As I have said, they are supposed to have been drawn up, with all the Biblical phraseology and references as here given, at the small imperial town of Memmngen, in March, 1525, and it is further supposed, though this is somewhat uncertain, that they are at least mainly from the pen of the Swiss pastor, Schappeler, who is known to have been present at the conference at Memmingen, and who was one of the most prominent advocates of the peasant cause in south Germany. But .although this was the usual form and content of the "Twelve Articles," and a form which seems to have been everywhere the most popular, it may be mentioned that it was supplemented, and perhaps in one or two cases superseded, in certain districts by other versions. As among the most important of these variations we may note the twelve demands formulated by the peasants of Elsass-Lothringen. They have the merit of being short and to the point, and divested of all sermonising, and are as follows:

1. Gospel shall be preached according to the true faith.

2. No tithes shall be given — neither great nor small.

3. There shall be no longer interest and no longer dues, more than one gulden in twenty (five per cent.)

4. All waters shall be free.

5. All woods and forests shall be free.

6. All game shall be free.

7. None shall any longer be in a state of villeinage.

5. None shall obey any longer any prince or lord, but such as pleaseth him, and that shall be the emperor.

9. Justice and right shall be as of old time.

10. Should there be one having authority who displeaseth us, we would have the power to set up in his place another as it pleaseth us.

11. There shall be no more death-dues.

12. The common lands which the lords have taken to themselves shall again become common lands.

The idea of there being no lord but the emperor, at the time very popular amongst constitutional reformers, here finds direct expression. The articles, it will be noticed, are also more drastic than those given in the classical version.

The movement was frequently inaugurated in a village by the reading of the "Twelve Articles" in the ale-house or wine-room, or it might be in the open air. They were everywhere received with acclamation, and the able-bodied among the villagers usually formed themselves straightway into a fighting contingent of the "Evangelical Brotherhood".

The "Twelve Articles" proper, as will be seen, were exclusively agrarian in character; they dealt with the grievances of the peasant against his lord, lay or ecclesiastic, but had nothing to say on the social problems and the ideas of political reconstruction agitating the mind of the landless proletarian or the impoverished handicraftsman within the walls of the towns. The many small, and, according to our notions, even diminutive, townships spread over central and southern Germany had, it is true, many points of contact with the agrarian revolution, but they none the less had their own special point of view, which was also in the main that of the larger towns. As we already know, every town had its Ehrbarkeit or patriciate, which often monopolised the seats of the council (Rath) and all the higher municipal offices. Many towns, even among the small ones above referred to, had a discontented section of poor guildsmen, and most had a proportionately larger or smaller contingent of precariously employed proletarians, who had either no municipal status at all, or who had at best to content themselves with that form of bare citizenship which conferred on them and theirs no more than the mere right of residence. The fact of living within fortified town walls, however small the area they enclosed, seemed itself to have the effect of creating a distinction between the townsman and the dweller in the open country, who in time of war had at best to secure his family and possessions in the fortified churchyard of his village. Hence, in spite of the strong bond of sympathy and common interest between the poor townsman and the peasant — a sympathy which as soon as the agrarian movement had begun to make headway showed solid fruits — it is clear that a programme that might suffice for the latter would not for the former. No sooner, therefore, did the towns begin to play a serious part in the revolutionary movement that the peasantry had inaugurated, than we find entering into it the new elements of a political, and, in some cases, of a religious-utopian character, elements which we fail to observe in the great peasant charter, the "Twelve Articles" itself, and only sporadically in the other subsidiary and local agrarian programmes.

Among the projects of political revolution to which the year 1525 gave birth, the foremost place is occupied by the "Evangelical Divine Reformation" of the empire, sketched out by two men, both of them townsmen of position and education, by name Wendel Hipler and Friedrich Weigand. These men embodied in their scheme, in definite form, the average aspirations of the revolutionary classes of the towns. As we have seen, the idea of centralisation and of an equality based on a bureaucratic constitution was present in the spurious reformation of Friedrich III., as in all the new political tendencies of the tine. As was only to be expected, it entered into the general revolutionary scheme drawn up by the two men above named and designed to be laid before the projected congress of peasant and town delegates to be held at Heilbronn. They both of them had held office at feudal courts. Wendel Hipler had been chancellor and secretary to the Count of Hohenlohe and chief clerk to the Palatinate. Friedrich Weigand had been a prominent court functionary of the archbishop of Mainz. They both threw themselves energetically into the new movement. Their marked intellectual superiority and practical knowledge of tactics is shown by their endeavours to effect a union on the basis of a definite plan of action between the various peasant encampments, as also in their conceptions of the proper position to take up towards their princely and ecclesiastical adversaries. The aim of Hipler and Weigand, as of most contemporary political reformers, was to strengthen the power of the emperor at the expense of the feudal estates. Weigand, whilst supporting the general view of compelling princes and lords to humble themselves to become simple members of the Evangelical League, conceived the idea of specially enlisting the lower nobility- and the towns against the princes. It is probable enough that this project was debuted in the standing committee of the movement, which sat during the greater part of its course at the imperial town of Heilbronn, and of which Hipler and Weigand were members, but respecting the proceedings of which we have little information. Weigand appears also to have broached the idea of an agreement being arrived at by a remodelled Reichregiment, manned by representatives of the lower nobility, of the towns, and of the peasantry.

The actual scheme of reconstruction drawn up by these two men was based upon the "Reformation of Kaiser Friedrich III." The language in which it is couched is studiously moderate, but the Biblical and pietistic phraseology of the "Twelve Articles" is almost entirely wanting. Whilst it embraces the agrarian demands of the peasants, these are merely incorporated as an element in the general scheme of reform. The stress is laid on the political side of things — on the notions of equality before the law, of reformed administration, and of national or imperial unity. The secularisation of the empire is insisted on; the ecclesiastical property is to be confiscated to the benefit of all needy men and of the common good. Priests or pastors are to be chosen by the community. They are to receive a seemly stipend, but are to be excluded from all political or juridical functions. Princes and lords are to be reformed in the sense that the poor man should be no longer oppressed by them. At the same time, a distinction between the estates was not to be entirely abolished. In this case, as in that of the "Twelve Articles," the moderation or opportunism of the official document is noteworthy when contrasted with the more sweeping and radical measures which were demanded in definite form by certain of the men and sections of the revolutionary party, and which, especially in northern and central Germany, seemed at times to animate the whole movement. In the Wendel Hipler project, indeed, a fourfold social division of the empire is proposed, consisting of (1) princes, counts and barons; (2) knights and squires; (3) townships; (4) rural communities. Equal justice is to be meted out to all. But princes and barons, while retaining their nominal rank, shall cease to possess independent power and shall hold their positions merely as functionaries and servants of the emperor, the medieval representative of German unity. As a necessary consequence, all rights of treaty, of jurisdiction, of coinage, or of levying tolls, appertaining to the separate estates, as such, shall cease to exist. An imperial coinage is to be established, with separate mints in different parts of the empire, bearing, in all cases, on the obverse the imperial eagle, and only on the reverse the armorial bearings of the prince or town within whose territory the particular mint happens to be situated. Customs dues, passage dues, direct and indirect taxes of every description are to cease. The emperor alone shall every ten years have the right of taxation. Justice is to be thoroughly reformed throughout the empire. Below the supreme court of the empire, the Kammergericht, are to be four subordinate courts; below these, four territorial courts; below these again four so-called "free courts, the administrative basis of the whole being the courts or open tribunals of the township and of the village-community. Whilst the higher judicial functions are allowed to be retained by the nobility and their assessors, every tribunal, from the highest to the lowest, is to be maimed by sixteen persons, judges and jurors. Doctors of the Roman law are to be rigidly excluded from judicial functions and restricted to lecturing on their science at the universities. A thorough reform, in a democratic sense, of township and communal government is postulated. All mortgages on land are to be redeemable on a payment down of a sum amounting to twenty years' interest.

Such are the leading features of the reform project drawn up by Wendel Hipler and Friedrich

Weigand for the consideration of the delegates from the townships and villages which should have come together in the month of June at Heilbronn. The congress in question was destined never to take place. The whole movement was, at the time it should have been held, in a state of imminent collapse, even in those districts where it had not already been crushed.

More agrarian and far more drastic in its revolutionary character was the plan of reform put forward by Michael Gaismayr, the intellectual leader of the revolt in Tyrol, in the Archbishopric of Salzburg, and in the Austrian hereditary territories generally. Michael Gaismayr, who was the son of a squire of Sterzing, had been secretary to the Bishop of Brixen. As soon as matters began to stir in the regions of the Eastern Alps, Gaismayr threw himself into the movement and ultimately became its chief. But it is noteworthy that, radical as were the demands he put forward, neither his activity nor his scheme of reform extended far outside the Tyrol and the neighhbouring territories. This being the case, it is only natural that his revolutionary plans should be mainly of an agrarian type. All castles and all town-walls and fortifications were to be levelled with the ground, and henceforth there were to be no more towns, but only villages, to the end that no man should think himself better than his neighbour. A strong central government was to administer public affairs. There was to be one university at the seat of government, which was to devote itself exclusively to Biblical studies. The calling of the merchant was to be forbidden, so that none might besmirch themselves with the sin of usury. On the other hind, cattle-breeding, husbandry, vine-culture, the draining of marshes, and the reclaiming of waste lands were to be encouraged; nay, were to constitute the exclusive occupations of the inhabitants of the countries concerned. All this is to a large extent an outcome of the general tendency of medieval communistic thought, with its Biblical colouring, and would-be resuscitation of primitive Christian conditions, or what were believed to have been such. It is the true development of the tradition of the English Lollards, and still more directly of the Bohemian Taborites.

The classical expression, however, of the religious-utopian side of the Peasants War, and, indeed, of the closing period of the Middle ages generally, is to be found in the doctrines and social theory of Thomas Münzer, which played so great a part in the Thuringian revolt, especially in the town of Mühlhausen, and which subsequently formed the theoretical basis of the anabaptist rising, as exemplified in the "kingdom of God in Münster. Since, however, we shall devote a special chapter to the Thuringian episode of the Peasants War, with particular reference to Thomas Münzer and his career, it is unnecessary to deal at length with it here. It is sufficient to say that if in the political plan of constitution formulated by Hipler and Weigand we have more especially the revolution as it presented itself to the mind of the townsman — just as in the Twelve Articles we have its formulation from the moderate peasant point of view, and in the scheme of Gaismayr the more radical expression of peasant aspirations as voiced by a man of education and intellectual capacity — so in the doctrines of it Münzer we have both sides of the movement fused and presented in the guise of a religious utopia, on the traditional lines of mediaeval communism, but of a more thoroughgoing and systematic character, the elaboration of which, however, was reserved for Münzer's anabaptist successors.

In the town-movement, as exemplified in the Hipler-Weigand scheme, the stress of which was political, the main ideas are on the lines of the then trend of historic evolution — i.e., towards centralisation and bureaucratic administration, equality before the law, etc. On the other hand. the distinctively peasant programme, as Lasalle has pointed out, was in the main reactionary, harking back as it did to the old village community with its primitive communistic basis, an institution which was destined to pass away in the natural course of economic development. The old group-holding of land, with communal property generally, was necessarily doomed to he gradually superseded by those individualistic rights of property that form the essential condition of the modern capitalist world.

In addition to the men who may be considered as the intellectual chiefs of the social revolt, we must not ignore the influence of those who were primarily religious reformers or sectaries, but who, notwithstanding, took sides with the social movement and formed a powerful stimulus throughout its course. The influence of the new religious doctrines, and of many of their preachers on the current of affairs is unmistakable to the most casual student of the period. As prominent types of this class of agitator, two names may be taken — that of Andreas Bodenstein, better known from his birthplace as Karlstadt, and that of Balthasar Hubmayer. The first-named was born at Karlstadt, Franconia, about 1483, was educated in Rome and became a Professor of Theology at Wittenberg. Drawn into the vortex of the Lutheran movement at an early age, he soon developed into a partisan of the extreme sects, and of the social doctrines which almost invariably accompanied them. Karlstadt, who was somewhat older than Luther, was twice rector of his university, besides being canon and archdeacon of the celebrated Stifskirche at Wittenberg. He it was who in his official capacity conferred the degree of doctor upon Luther. Karlstadt enjoyed general esteem in the university. Though at first he was closely identified with Luther, the objects of the two men were probably different even at the outset. Luther was only concerned with the freeing of the soul; the theological interest with him outweighed every other. Karlstadt, on the contrary, though primarily a theologian, was still more concerned for the bodily welfare of his fellow- Christians and for the establishment of a system of righteousness in this world. Luther had always regarded the authorities as his mainstay Karlstadt appealed to the people. In theology and ecclesiastical matters as in social views, Karlstadt was essentially revolutionary, while Luther was the mere reformer. Finally, the tendency of Luther was to become more conservative or opportunist with years, while, on the contrary, Karlstadt became more revolutionary. As Luther placed the Bible above Church tradition, Karlstadt placed the inner light of the soul above the Bible. Indeed, in his utterances respecting the latter, he anticipated many of the points of modern criticism.

While Luther was in the Wartburg, the mystics of Zwichau, the friends of Thomas Münzer came to Wittenberg. This was the turning-point with Karlstadt. Carried away by these enthusiasts, a new world seemed to open up before him. Theology lost its importance; life and political action became all in all. He now rejected all human learning as worthless and injurious; in the dress of a peasant or handicraftsman he went now among the people. That man should throw off all learning, all human authority, and should return to natural conditions, became henceforth his central teaching. In fact, his was the Rousseauite doctrine before its time. In fanatical iconoclasm he had scarcely an equal.

At length he was compelled to leave Wittenberg. He repaired to the farm of his father-in-law and worked as a labourer. The life of the husbandman and the handicraftsman he proclaimed as the only worthy one. He demanded that all ecclesiastical goods should be confiscated for the benefit of the poor. This new departure naturally offended Luther, and the inevitable rupture between the two men occurred nn Luther's return to Wittenlerg. Eventually, Karlstadt betook himself first to

Orlamunda and then to Rothenburg on the Tauber, just as the revolutionary movement was beginning there, into which he energetically threw himself. He was subsequently compelled to conceal himself in the houses of friends in the town, escaping the hot pursuit of the reaction by letting himself down by a rope, at night from the city wall.

Balthasar Hubmayer, born in the Bavarian town of Friedberg, near Augsburg, in the last quarter of the fifteenth century, began as a learned theologian, and after teaching at the University of Friedberg become pro-rector of the University of Ingolstadt. He was then made chief preacher of the cathedral at Regensburg, where he initiated an anti-Jewish campaign, which resulted in the invasion of the Jewish quarter of the town and the total demolition of the synagogue. On the site of the latter a chapel was built in honour of the "fair Mary," the image contained in which had the reputation of effecting miraculous cures. Popular excitement caused by this led to a scandal (see German Society, pp.268-271). This was in the year 1516. Shortly after the outbreak of the Reformation, being attracted by the latter, he left his post at Regensburg and became preacher in the little town of Waldshut on the borders of the Black Forest. About the same time, he made the acquaintance of Zwingli and the Swiss reformers, and soon assumed the character of an energetic apostle of the new doctrines. The citizens of Waldshut, together with the clergy of the town and surrounding districts, acclaimed him with enthusiasm. He became the hero and prophet of Waldshut. Such was his success in his new capacity that the Austrian authorities at Ensisheim, the seat of the Austrian Government in south-west Germany, became alarmed, and demanded the extradition of the popular preacher us a dangerous agitator. This was refused by the town. Hubmayer, however, insisted upon leaving "to the end that no man may be prejudiced or injured on my account, and that ye may preserve rest and peace ". Accordingly, on the 17th of August, 1524, accompanied by the blessings and plaudits of the townsfolk, he rode out of the eastern gate. A small body of armed men were in readiness to receive him from the hands of the Waldshuters, and to conduct him to the Swiss town of Schaffhausen, where he found safety and a favourable reception.

Meanwhile, as we have seen, Hans Müller von Bulgenbach, with his peasant bands, had fraternised with the people of Waldshut, and the Peasants War began to threaten. The result of the situation was that, notwithstanding hostile preparations, the Austrian Government found it prudent for a while to let Waldshut alone, more especially as the Swiss cantons of Schaffhausen and Zurich showed signs of moving in its favour. Emboldened by immunity, the Waldshuters recalled their favourite preacher. He was received, as an official document of the time states, "with drums, pipes and horns, and with such pomp as though he were the emperor himself". A great feast was given him in the guildhall, and general rejoicing followed. About this time either Thomas Münzer himself or some of his followers who were agitating in the Black forest districts, appear to have visited Waldshut. Hubmayer now became an enthusiastic partisan and apostle of the new social doctrines of the realisation of the Kingdom of God upon earth, in the shape of a Christian commonwealth based on equality of status and community of goods. Hubmayer threw himself with renewed zeal into the agitation for the cause to which he had been won over by Münzer or his disciples.

The clergy more especially showed themselves receptive for the new doctrines. In fact, we have taken Karlstadt and Hubmayer as the most eminent types of a class of reforming priest — reforming in a social and political no less than in a theological sense — which at the time of which we write had numerous representatives throughout Germany. All developments of the social movement found their advocates among the revolted priesthood the moderate and immediate demands of the peasants as expressed in the official Twelve Articles, the political and administrative reformation of the empire upon which the Hipler-Weigand scheme lays so much stress, and, perhaps more than all, the religious-economic utopianism of which Thomas Münzer was the leading exponent.

Notes

1. Uemeinde in the original. This means, of course, the "rural community" of the village or district. It might be translated "commune," or in some cases even loosely as "parish," though the old English "hundred" probably answers most nearly to it.

Chapter IV. The Movement in South Germany

THE heads of the Swabian League sitting in the imperial town of Ulm were glad enough to keep up the force of negotiations with the peasants, in accordance with the principle already- laid down by the Archduke of Austria, namely, that of quieting them with promises and vague hopes until preparations for taking the field should be completed. Truchsess, the head of the military forces of the League, was meanwhile straining every nerve to get fighting men to join his standard. As a contemporary manuscript expressly has it, "they kept the peasants at bay- with words so long as they could, and armed meanwhile to attack them". But the Landesknechte employed by Truchsess were inclined to be mutinous. Their pay was in arrears, and they were especially indisposed to take the field against the peasants, the class from which most of them sprung, and whose grievances they well appreciated. Still, by dint of threats, promises and money, Truchsess at length succeeded in getting together a force of 8,000 foot and 3,000 horse. By the end of March the peasants, on their side, began to weary of the interminable negotiations with the League at Ulm, whose object was now only too apparent, and determined to begin active operations. Truchsess, fearing lest the body encamped in the district known as the Ried, and called from its place of origin the "Baltringer contingent," might cut off his retreat to his own castle and domains and possibly invade them, determined to attach this section first. His relations with his own tenants seem to have been can the whole fairly good, and he appears to have left his family at the Waldsee.

As we have already seen, the Baltringer or Ried contingent formed one of the three sections of the "Evangelical Peasant Brotherhood," the other two being the Black Forest and the Lake contingents. But in the marshy district where the Baltringer division was encamped, Truchsess could not transport his heavy guns easily nor manoeuvre his cavalry with effect. All he could do, therefore, was to send a detachment of foot under Frowen Von Hutten to attack them. The peasants retired to a favourable position in the hope of inducing Truchsess to risk his whole force on the treacherous ground. He remained, however, where he was, contenting himself with sending out a foraging party which plundered a few villages, but which was eventually cut off by a body of peasants and its members either killed or driven back into their camp. The object the leader of the Swabian army had in view was to draw the main peasant force into firm open country and compel them to engage in a pitched battle, knowing that under such circumstances they would be at a hopeless disadvantage. To this end he sent sundry spies in the form of messengers into the peasant camp, but the insurgents, though they answered peaceably, proceeded to entrench themselves still more securely behind a wood. The peasants further endeavoured to induce Truchsess's free-lances to desert to their camp by means of secret negotiations. They were, they said, their sons and brothers, and this, in fact, was the case. Most of the foot-soldiery of the time was recruited out of poor town proletarians or impoverished peasants' sons, who, in many cases as a last resort, had taken to the trade of arms and were prepared to serve any muster for a few hellers a day and the hope of booty. But, although this was their only chance of victory — to induce experienced fighting men to enter their ranks — many of their number were averse to being led by, or even to having in their company, any free-lances. The peasant leaders were partly jealous of the latter's superiority in war to themselves, while many of the rank and file dreaded their dissolute habits, for which they had an evil notoriety. Wendel Hipler and the far-seeing heads of the movement strove in vain to effect an understanding between the free-lances and the peasants. Their ways of life were different, and, though both belonged to the people, a certain mutual distrust could not be surmounted.

Finally, after a short and indecisive passage of arms with the main Baltringer contingent, Truchsess withdrew his forces in the direction of the little town of Leipheim, in the neighbourhood of which an important detachment of insurgents was commanded by the preacher Jakob Wehe. Wehe was an enthusiastic upholder of the peasant claims, and a prudent and energetic leader in action. He had already constituted a war-chest and a reserve fund. A train of sixty waggons containing provisions and material of war, followed his detachment, which, in spite of the admonitions of their leader, showed itself not averse to excesses. The worthy priest had as his goal to unite with two other bodies encamped not far distant, to march on Ulm, and to seize that important Imperial city, the seat of the heads of the Swabian league, whose patrician council had moreover, shown itself so unsympathetic to the popular cause. His immediate objective, however, was the town of Weissenhorn. In Weissenhorn, as in all the towns, the wealthier guildsmen all the patriciate were on the side of the Swabian League. A garrison of 340 horsemen had been hastily thrown into the town by the Count Palatine. The gates were remorselessly shut against the peasants, the utmost concession made being the passing of bread and wine over the wall. Hearing of the near approach of Truchsess, and aware of the hopelessness of attempting to withstand his cavalry charge in the open field, Wehe decided to retreat on Leipheim; where he had entrenchements.

On the following clay a detachment stormed the castle of Roggenburg, making themselves drunk on the contents of the wine-cellars. In this condition they destroyed the church, with its organ and costly plate, making hands for their hose out of the church banners and vestments. One of their number donned the chasuble and biretta of the Abbot off Roggenburg, and, seated on the altar, made his comrades do him homage. This besotted jesting went on the whole day. Another detachment, also on plunder bent, was cut off by some horsemen of the league and partly destroyed and partly taken prisoners to Ulm.

Jakob Wehe, anxious to gain time, sent by a trusty messenger the following letter to the council of the league at Ulm:-

"As warriors of understanding and experience, ye will easily see that the assembly of peasants waxeth ever greater with time, and that such a multitude may not readily be compelled. That which hath happened that is unmete doth with truth grieve us and our brethren in other places, who have been innocently moved thereto, but to the end that further mischief may be prevented, we entreat that the league shall be a true furtherer of God's glory and of peace. We will also ourselves, so far as in us lies, zealously do our utmost with other assemblies that complaints should be heard by God-fearing and understanding men, who hate time-serving and love the common weal, and that all grievances shall he made straight in peace and by judicial decisions."

The above letter had scarcely reached Ulm before "Herr George" with his army- was already within sight of Leipheim. Here the peasants were entrenched 3,000 strong. The town was already in their possession. The camp was some distance outside and had on its right the river, on its left the wood. Its front was covered by a marsh, and behind it was a barricade of waggons. A vanguard of horsemen was kept at bay, but, as soon as the peasants saw Thruchsess with his whole army advancing on them, they decided to retreat within the walls to await reinforcements. The retreat was only partially successful. The peasants carried indeed their dead and wounded with them and buried the former in a ditch by the roadside. About 2,000 succeeded in reaching Leipheim, whilst about 1,000 were either driven into the Danube and drowned or cut down in the field. Truchsess now made direct for Leipheim, which he decided to storm. The inhabitants, however, lost courage, sending an old man and some women to beg for mercy. The general of the league forces answered that they must surrender themselves at discretion, and first of all hand over to him their pastor and captain, Jakob Wehe, terms which were agreed to. No sooner did Wehe see the turn things had taken than, gathering together some 200 florins, he bethought himself of escape. His parsonage was built against the town wall, whence a secret subterranean passage led under the wall down to the Danube. of this he availed himself in the company of a friend and succeeded in reaching a cave known to him in a rock in the banks of the river, where he remained in hiding. The town was entered, but under conditions causing great discontent to a portion of Truchsess's men, for the freelances were not allowed to plunder as they had been promised in the event of the town being taken by storm. On Wednesday, the 5th of April, the neighbouring town of Günzhurg which had also gone with the peasants, capitulated to the league, having to pay in all a ransom amounting to 1,000 gold gulden. Three of the leaders taken prisoners at Leipheim and four at Günzhurg were condemned to death.

Meanwhile, search was made everywhere for Jakob Wehe in vain, until his whereabouts were disclosed to some freelances by the barking of a dog outside his retreat. The offer of the 200 florins he had with him proved of no avail to free him. His captors took him bound on a hurdle to their master at I>ul>esheim, where he was condemned to share the fate of the seven other captives spoken of above. On the 5th of April towards evening, they were taken to a flowery meadow lying between Leipheim and Bubesheim to be executed. As Master Jakob was led forward to the block, Truchsess turned to him with the words "Sir pastor, it had been well for thee and us hadst thou preached God's word, as it beseemeth, and not rebellion "Noble sir," answered the preacher, "ye do me wrong. I have not preached rebellion, but God's word." "I am otherwise informed," observed Truchsess, as his chaplain stepped forward to receive the confession of the condemned man. Weke turned to those around, stating that he had already confessed to his Maker and commended his soul to Him. To his fellow-sufferers he observed: "Be of good cheer, brethren, we shall yet meet each other to-day in Paradise, for when our eyes seem to close, they are really first opening". After having prayed aloud, concluding with the words: "Father, forgive them, for they know not what they do," he laid himself on the block, and in another moment his head fell in the long grass.

The preacher of Münzhurg, who had also taken part in the movement, and an old soldier of fortune, who had joined the rebels, were brought forward in their turn to submit to the same fate, when the old soldier, turning to Truchsess, observed: "Doth it not seem to thee a little late in the day, noble lord, for one to lose one's head?" This humorous observation saved the lives of himself and the preacher. The latter was carried about with the troops in a cage, until he had bought his freedom with eighty gulden. He lost, however, the right of preaching and of riding on horseback!

Meanwhile, the free-lances of "Herr George" were becoming more mutinous every day. They held not made the booty they expected, and their pay was long outstanding. The danger to the commander's own castles — notably the Waldburg or Waldsee, where his wife and child resided — was imminent. Still the freelances would not budge. Some of his noble colleagues and neighbours took the matter in hand and occupied his territories. It was, however, too late. The Waldsee had capitulated to the Baltringer and bought itself off for 4000 gulden. The attacking party did not know that the countess and her child were located within, or it would probably have gone badly with them. In the course of a few days, the League having undertaken to pay the month's arrears of wages, the matter with the free-lances was arranged.

The peasants, however, were by no means disheartened by the check that their cause had received at Leipheim. Truchsess, with a force of double their number, including cavalry, and well-equipped with artillery, might succeed in crushing one holy, but, with his eight or nine thousand men, he could not be everywhere at the same time. A few days after, Truchsess eagerly seized an opportunity of negotiating a truce with the so-called Lake continent and the Hegauers, which relieved him for the moment and of which we shall have occasion to speak later on. Just at this juncture the movement was rapidly reaching its height. It was computed that no fewer than 300,000 peasants, besides necessitous townsfolk, were armed and in open rebellion. On the side of the nobles, no adequate force was ready to meet the emergency. In every direction were to be seen flaming castles and monasteries. On all sides were bodies of armed country-folk, organised in military fashion, dictating their will to the countryside and the small towns, whilst disaffection was beginning to show itself in a threatening manner among the popular elements of not a few important cities. The victory of the league at Leipheim had done nothing to improve the situation from the point of view of the governing powers. In Easter week, 1525, it looked indeed as if the "Twelve Articles," at least, would become realised, if not the Christian Commonwealth dreamed of by the religious sectaries established throughout the length and breadth of Germany. Princes, lords and ecclesiastical dignitaries were being compelled far and wide to save their lives, after their property was probably already confiscated, by swearing allegiance to the Christian League or Brotherhood of the peasants and by countersigning the Twelve Articles and other demands of their refractory villeins and serfs. So threatening was the situation that the Archduke Ferdinand began himself to yield in so far as to enter into negotiations with the insurgents. These were mostly carried on through the intermediary of a certain Walther Bach, One of the peasant leaders in the Allgau and an ex-soldier in the Austrian service. The only result, however, was that Walther Bach fell under the suspicion of his followers and was shortly afterwards deposed from his position by them.

In brilliancy of get-up, none equalled Hans Müller from Bulgenbach and his two colleagues,

Hans Eitel and Johann Zügelmuller, and their followings. We read of purple mantles and scarlet birettas with ostrich plumes as the costume of the leaders, of a suite of men in scarlet dress, of a vanguard of ten heralds gorgeously attired. This combined contingent of the Black Forest and surrounding districts went from one success to another, taking castle after castle, including as before mentioned that of Lupfen, the seat of the Countess Helena of "snail-shell" notoriety, which was the alleged proximate guise of the insurrection. After leaving peasant garrisons in all the places captured, Hans Müller bethought himself attacking Radolfzell, where, as we have seen, a considerable number of nobles and clergy had taken refuge. He does not seem, however, to have immediately attempted any formal siege of the town, but simply to have cut off all communications and laid waste the surrounding country. Indeed, as is truly observed by Lamprecht (Deutsche Geschichte, vol. v., p. 343), "the peasant revolts were, in general, less of the nature of campaigns, or even of an uninterrupted series of minor military operations, than of a slow process of mobilisation, interrupted and accompanied by continual negotiations with the lords and princes — a mobilisation which was rendered possible by the standing right of assembly and of carrying arms possessed by the peasants".

The duchy of Würtemberg, the home of the "poor Conrad," was, as we have seen, ripe for insurrection at the time of Duke Ulrich's abortive attempt to regain possession of his coronet. While Truchsess was operating about Leipheim and holding the Baltringer contingent at bay, the Würtemberg authorities, spiritual and temporal, found themselves face to face with a threatening peasant population, everywhere gathering under arms. The assembly of the estates of the duchy had been called together at Stuttgart to deliberate on the matter. The result was the immediate despatch of an embassy to Ulm to represent their case to the council of the Swabian League. The latter replied sympathetically, but observed that the regency of the archduke and the estates themselves were largely to blame for the position of affairs, pointing out that, while every member of the league was by the terms of its oath obliged to keep its most important castles and towns in a state of thorough defensive repair, in Würtemberg there was not a single castle which was capable of holding out, and that the frontiers especially were entirely exposed. All that they could promise was that, as soon as Truchsess had settled affairs in Upper Swabia, he should come to their assistance. The allegations were quite true; the duchy was absolutely denuded of fighting men through the Italian war, the archduke having taken no care or having been unable to replace those; he had sent to his brother with any other sufficient force. The finances of the country, bad as they had been before, were now almost entirely exhausted by the resistance to Duke Ulrich's invasion. Turning from the league to the archduke, the estates were similarly met by promises, but no assistance way forthcoming.

Meanwhile, the small towns were everywhere opening their gates without resistance to the peasants, between whom and the poorer inhabitants an understanding usually existed. Here as elsewhere, defenceless castles were falling into the hands of the insurgents, who waxed fat with plunder, and in many cases drink themselves senseless with the contents of rich monastic wine-cellars. In the valley of the Neckar an innkeeper, named Matern Feuerbacher, was chosen as captain of the popular forces. Feuerbacher was compelled to accept the leadership of the insurgents against his will. The nobles in the vicinity of the small town of Bottwar, where Feuerbacher had his inn, knew him well as an honest good-natured person, with whom they even at times conversed, as they sat in his wine-room, and they were by no means averse to the choice the insurgents had made. The innkeeper at first hid himself on the approach of the peasant delegates, who threatened his wife that if her husband did not, on their next demand, consent to place himself at their head, they would plant the ominous stake, denoting his outlawry before his door.

Just at this time an event occurred at the little town of Weinsberg, of "faithful wife" fame, near the free imperial city of Heilbronn to the north of the duchy, which constituted a landmark in the history of the peasant rising. The town proletariat of Heilbronn had been stirring from February onwards, and by the end of March a good understanding had been arrived at between them and the peasantry of the surrounding country. The leader of the movement here was one Jakob Rohrbach, commonly called by the nick-name of "Jäcklein Rohrbach," or sometimes simply "Jäcklein". He kept an inn in a village called Bockingen, a short distance from Heilbronn. He is described as young, well-built, and strong, of burgher descent, and intelligent withal. His reputation as a boon companion was immense, and as he was of a generous nature and treated freely, his popularity, especially with the young people of the district, was enormous. Always of a rebellious disposition, he had had many a tussle with constituted authority. The most serious appears to have been in 1519, when he was accused of stabbing the head man of his village, against whom he had a grievance. For this he was to be arrested and tried, but threatened the constable and the judges that, if they dared to lay hands upon him, the whole place should be burnt to the ground. Knowing that all the countrymen of the neighbourhood were on his side and would very probably put this threat into execution, or, at best, avenge themselves in some other unpleasant way, the local authorities found it prudent to let the matter drop. Jäcklein Rohrbach, in short, was the terror of all respectable persons.

His chief companions were the sons of the peasantry, whom he saw oppressed on all sides. A village girl, with whom he was in love, was seized by the forest ranger of a neighbouring lord for gathering wild strawberries, maltreated and subsequently ravished. This may have given a deeper colour to his hatred of the aristocrat. In any case, by the end of 1324, Jäcklein found his money spent and himself in an apparently hopeless condition economically. At the wine time, his hatred of the existing order of society knew no bounds. An ecclesiastic had sought to obtain payment of a debt from Jäcklein. The latter had assembled his peasants at Bockingen, and had, in addition, called out some of the town proletarians from Heilbronn in order to prevent the hearing of the case. On the demand of the priest, the council of Heilbronn sent one of their number to Bockingen, who speedily returned with the news that the village was full of armed men at the service of Rohrbach. The council, thereupon, advised the clergyman to let his plaint fall for the time being, as his pursuing it would only lead to a disturbance, which for the moment there was no means of quelling. This was at the end of March. On the 2nd of April, Rohrbach, who had the previous day repaired with his following to the village of Flein, also in the Heilbronn territory, raised the standard of revolt, and soon had 300 more supporters from the neighbouring villages around him. He had been long in communication with Wendel Hipler and George Metzler, a leader of the Odenwald insurgents, of whom we shall speak presently. Jäcklein was now strong enough to compel by threats, or otherwise, the neighbouring places to supply him with men to serve under his standard. As soon as he had gathered together 1,500 partisans, he proceeded to join the main body of insurgents in the Schonthal, under the leadership of Metzler. The body was known as the "Heller Haufen," which may be translated as the "United Contingent" In the meantime, the bold Jäcklein had seized the head-man of Bockingen, thrown him into prison, and set up a new one of his own choosing. As a taste of the good things in store for them, he had also allowed his men to fish out a small lake belonging to a patrician councillor of Heilbronn.

George Metzler, the commander of the "United Contingent" had been from the beginning of the movement a zealous agitator and organiser. He was an innkeeper in the town of Balenberg, and his wine-room was the resort of all the discontented and insurrectionary elements of the neighbouring districts. As soon as the Swabians had begun to move, Metzler bound a peasant's shoe (the Bundschuh) to a pole and carried it about the country, preceded by a man beating a drum. In a short time he had 2000 men around his "shoe". This body, which steadily increased, was given a form of military organisation by Wendel Hipler (the peasants Chancellor), who now appeared upon the scene, and Metzler was definitely appointed its commander. Thus, while some of the other contingents were little better than hordes, the Heller Haufen assumed more the character of an army. It had its grades and its judiciary power, and in front of it was carried the "Twelve Articles," which all were required to swear to and to sign. Princes, bishops and nobles had the alternative offered them of loss of property or life, or of entrance into the Evangelical Brotherhood. The two Counts of Hohenlohe, the most considerable feudal potentates of the neighbourhood, received the challenge in question in the name of the "United Contingent". On their scornfully replying that they were ignorant to what order of animal the "United Contingent" might belong, Hipler is reported to have given the following rejoinder: "It is an animal that usually feedeth on roots and wild herbs, but which when driven by hunger sometimes consumeth priests, bishops and fat citizens. It is very old, but very strange it is that the older it becometh, by so much doth it wax in strength, even as with wine. The beast doth all at times, but it never dieth. At times, too, it forsaketh the land of its birth for foreign parts, but early or late it returneth home again". "Tell my lords, the counts," added Hipler, it is said, to the envoys who brought him the message, "that it is even now come again into Germany, and that at this hour it pastureth in the Schupfer valley." On the foregoing message being returned to them, the counts seem to have given way. The two brothers, Albrecht and George, met the delegates of the "United Contingent," now 8,000 strong, in the open air, and after some negotiations, during which they endeavoured to persuade the peasants to submit their grievances to a judicial tribunal, they were compelled to swear to the "Twelve Articles". This they were required to do with uplifted hands and to remove their gloves, whilst the peasants, on the contrary, retained theirs (probably assumed for the occasion). By this oath, the Counts were admitted into the Evangelical Brotherhood.

But these things did not create that profound impression which constituted the landmark in the Peasants War before spoken of. It was the celebrated "blood-vengeance" of the peasants in the township of Weinsberg, near Heilbronn, that did so. Weinsberg, with its castle, had been occupied, by the orders of the Archduke, by Count Ludwig von Helfenstein, whose wife was the illegitimate daughter of the Emperor Maximilian and therefore half-sister to the Emperor Charles and to his brother Ferdinand. This Helfenstein, who was a young man of twenty-seven, had seen fifteen years' service in war and had recently shown himself very active in killing peasants, wherever he found them isolated or in small bands. His recent journey to Weinsberg had been signalised by several acts of this description. A number of the citizens of the little town were inclined to open the gates to "the enemy". As a body of peasants appeared before the town demanding admission, Helfenstein without any parley made a sortie with his knights and men-at-arms and massacred them in cold blood. As he heard this, Jäcklein Rohrbach is said to have exclaimed: "Death and hell! We shall know how to avenge ourselves on Count Helfenstein for his mode of warfare!" It must be admitted, indeed, that for this act alone Helfenstein richly deserved the fate which afterwards befel him.

On the same day, news arrived in the camp of the "United Contingent" that the brothers, the Courts of Hohenlohe, had refused to supply the force with the pieces of artillery for which it had applied to them and which it so urgently needed. This, coming immediately after the report of Jahob Wehe's execution at Leipheim, excited the indignation of the insurgents against the nobles to fever pitch. The counts had solemnly sworn to maintain and further the peasant cause, and this refusal of theirs to supply the ordnance required was seen in the light of an act of treachery. Jäcklein Rohrbach moved that a sufficient force he sent to storm and enter "that nest of nobles," Weinsberg. The proposition was carried, as against that of going back to punish the Counts Hohenlohe, as some would have wished. Accordingly, a large body proceeded in the direction of Weinsberg by way of Neckarsal, which surrendered to them. After having pitched its camp, the "United Contingent" sent an ultimatum to the former town demanding unconditional surrender. Helfenstein returned a contemptuous answer, shortly after, the wife of a citizen came out to the peasants, urging them to the attack, and stating that half the inhabitants were with them and would open the gates. Another citizen offered to show them the weak points in the town-walls and in the castle.

On the 16th of April, the count and all the nobles at that time in Weinsberg were placed by the peasants under a ban. Helfenstein does not seem to have believed in a serious attack. He could not think that mere peasants would be so daring. He was awaiting the arrival of reinforcements from Stuttgart and from the Palatinate. Meanwhile, he employed his men in strengthening the weak parts of the fortifications. At break of day, the peasants moved forward from their encampment and established themselves on an eminence overlooking the town. For the last time, heralds were sent. They carried a hat upon a pole. "Open the gates," they cried, "open the town to the United Christian Band! If not, remove wife and child, for all that remains in the town must be put to the sword!" The only answer received was a shot from the walls, which wounded one of the heralds. He had just sufficient strength to crawl back into camp, and, fainting from loss of blood, to cry for vengeance. Within the walls of the township, the knights saddled their horses, and the free-lances made themselves ready. Only five men could be afforded for the defence of the castle, which contained Helfenstein's wife, child and valuables. The rest, not more than seventy or eighty all told, were necessary to defend the walls and gates. The count, with his knights and men-at-arms, appeared in the market-place and exhorted the assembled citizens to remain loyal to him, assuring them that help would come in the course of the day. Knights, citizens and men-at-arms thereupon repaired to the church — it being Easter Sunday — to hear mass and take the sacrament.

At nine o'clock, before the service was ended, the cry arose that the peasants were advancing on the town. The first to attack was the great Franconian hero of the Peasants War, the knight Florian Geyer — of whom we shall hear more presently his "black troop," who had come down from the north and effected a juncture with Metzler and the "United Contingent". The point of attack was the castle. Before the defenders had time to set themselves in readiness, a shout was heard front above, and two of Florian Geyer's banners waved from the battlements of the castle, which had been taken by storm. At the same moment, two of the town gates fell before the attach of Jächlein Rohrbach and his comrades. Many of the inhabitants assisted the storming party from within. In a moment, seeing the situation hopeless, Helfenstein sent a monk on to the wall who cried: "Peace, peace!" The only answer returned was: "Death and vengeance!" On hearing these cries, the count bethought himself of flight, but was surrounded by a body of citizens, cursing and threatening him for attempting to leave them in the lurch.

At this moment Jäcklein's storming party, mad with fury, dashed up the main street toward the market-place, shouting to the citizens to keep to their houses for that all nobles and men-at-arms were about to be put to death. The knights and men-at-arms had by this time fled into the church for protection, the count with eighteen nobles of his following escaping by a secret staircase into the church-tower. Jäcklein's comrades now burst into the churchyard, striking down lords and fighting men right and left. In a few minutes as many as forty had fallen. Finally, they discovered the secret staircase.

"Here we have them altogether," cried Jäcklein; "strike them all dead!" The knight Dietrich von Weller stepped forward on the gallery of the church tower, as the peasants burst in upon the fugitives, offering 30,000 gulden as ransom.

"An ye would offer us a tun-full of gold, yet should ye all die!" shouted the peasants with one consent. "Vengeance for the blood of our fallen brethren!"

At the next instant a musket shot laid him on the ground. A peasant them beat his brains out with a club. Others were compelled to spring from the top of the church tower, whence they were received on the spears of the peasants below. At last the main body of the "United Contingent" appeared upon the scene, under the command of George Metzler himself, who forthwith gave strict orders that the killing should discontinue, and that only prisoners should be taken. Helfenstein, with his wife and son, were seized, the child received a wound from a peasant as he was crossing the churchyard with his captors.

Jäcklein begged his leader to allow him and his troop the custody of his prisoners. This was accorded him. The order was now given that all who concealed a nobleman or a free-lance should be but to death. The result was that all were surrendered, with the exception of three, one of whom escaped in woman's clothes, whilst another concealed himself in a stove, and the third, a handsome young fellow, was hidden in a hayloft by a girl. Curiously enough, Jäcklein and some of his friends passed the night in this very hayloft, discussing the way in which they would bring about the slaughter of the prisoners taken.

The rank and file now demanded the right to plunder the town, but this was not conceded by Metzler and Hipler, who insisted upon only permitting the plunder of churches and monasteries and castles. In most cases, even where plundering was the order of the day, it was easy to hoodwink these naive children of the soil. Having, for instance, found a trunk full of gold in the Bürgermeister's house, the innocent countrymen were induced not to lay hands on it by a story that it was a chest the contents of which were destined for almsgiving purposes.

But to booty, drink and women the former boon companion, roisterer and spendthrift, Jäcklein Rohrbach, for the moment appeared indifferent. His whole soul seemed possessed by one idea — hatred and vengeance — vengeance on the privileged classes of the existing society. With this object always in view, he imprisoned his captives in a mill near the town wall, resolved to evade Metzler's orders and slay them, if possible, at break of day. Having ascertained that Metzler and the main body of the "United Contingent" were still sleeping after their heavy drinking bout of the previous evening, Jäcklein led his prisoners from the mill to a meadow outside the walls, hard by. They were eighteen in all, mostly knights, with a few free-lances and pages, foremost among them being of course the Count and Countess von Helfenstein and their two-year-old son. The men were all placed shoulder to shoulder in a semi-circle, and sentence of death was passed upon them by Jäcklein. It was decided that they should be compelled to "run the gauntlet". This was regarded as a degrading punishment, which was only applied to common soldiers of fortune guilty of some grave criminal offence against military honour. Accordingly, on a signal given by Jäcklein, a double row of spears was formed. Jäcklein then cried out: "Count Helfenstein, it is your turn to open the dance!" "Mercy exclaimed the countess, as with child in her arms she threw herself at Jäcklein's feet. "Thou pray'st for mercy for thy husband," cried he "it may not be!" Thereupon, he seized the countess by the arm, and throwing her back on the ground, knelt on her bosom, exclaiming "Behold, brethren, Jäcklein Rohrbach kneels on the emperor's daughter!" "Vengeance!" shouted the assembled peasants.

"Countess Helfenstein," cried one of their number, " thy horsemen, thy dogs and thy huntsmen have trodden down my fields. My boys opposed you. They were gagged and carried forth, as though they had been dogs themselves," and, uttering a cry of "Vengeance," he flung a knife at the countess. It struck the child in the arm, the blood spurting into its mother's face. "Mercy, mercy!" the woman continued to cry, as she rolled on the ground.

"Count Helfenstein," shouted another peasant, "thou hast thrust my brother into thy dungeon because, forsooth, he did not bare his head as thou passedst by! Thou shalt perish!" "Thou hast harnessed us like oxen to theyoke. Thou hast caused the hands of my father to be smitten off, for that he killed a hare on his own field," shouted another. " Thou hast wrung the last heller out of us," exclaimed several.

These and other accusations of a like kind, even if they may not all have been deserved strictly by Helfenstein himself, certainly were so by the feudal lords in general whose representative he on this occasion was. At last, the count himself was driven to beg for mercy at the hands of the peasant leader. He offered him his whole fortune and 60,000 gulden in addition, for which he was prepared to pledge the emperor's credit. He swore it on the head of his wife and son. It was now about half an hour before sunrise. "Not for 60,000 tuns of pearls," replied Jäcklein. "Kneel down and confess, for thou shalt never again behold the sun!"

"Only wait," cried Melchior Nonenmacher, a discharged piper of the count's, whose function it had been to play for him at his ancestral castle in Swabia during meals, but who now formed one of Jaclclein's bodyguard. "Long enough have I made table music for thee. I know thy favourite tune and have kept it for this thy last dance!" The piper thereupon proceeded to tune his instrument, whilst his former master confessed to a priest. As soon as he held finished the piper seized the count's hilt and domled it himself, and, dancing before him, whilst playing his favourite air, led the way to the double file of spears, through which he was condemned to pass. The countess was held upright by two men that she might see her husband fall.

Standing by and taking an active part in the scene was a woman known as the "black Hoffmann," a reputed witch, and one of the most striking dramatic figures of the Peasants War. She was, in respect of deep-seated, savage hatred of prince, noble and prelate, the female counterpart of Jäcklein, though her lust of vengeance was, if anything, of a deeper hue, and she seems to have lacked Jäcklein's original light-hearted generosity of disposition. Her dark shiny and jet-black hair probably gave her her name. She was the cast-off child of a wandering gipsy woman. Her mother had deserted her in Bockingen, in the native village, that is, of Jäcklein himself. Here she gained her living by tending cattle, a calling she subsequently abandoned for fortune-telling and kindred arts. She is described as the Egeria of Jäcklein, whose purpose she was continuously sharpening. She was usually clad in a black cloak and hood, with a red girdle or sash, the ends of which fluttered in the wind. As soon as Jäcklein had formed his band, she joined them as a kind of prophetess who presaged them victory, blessed their weapons, and urged them on to the fight. During the storming of Weinsberg, she had stood upon a neighbouring hill and with outstretched arms had ceaselessly shouted: "Down with the dogs; strike them all dead! Fear nothing! I bless your weapons I, the black Hoffmann! Only strike! God wills it!"

The hour of vengeance had now come. As the Count von Helfenstein fell beneath the peasants' spears, seizing a knife from her girdle this strange unsexed fury plunged it into his body, and proceeded to smear the shoes and lances of the peasants with the "fat ". In half an hour the last of the knights and men-at-arms had fallen. As the sun rose, the countess and her young son alone remained.

After Jäcklein and his partisans had distributed the clothes of the dead nobles amongst themselves, Jäcklein, who had himself assumed the garments of the count, addressed the countess and said: " In a golden chariot camest thou hither; in a dungcart shalt thou depart hence! Tell thine emperor this, and greet him from me!" To this she replied: "I have sinned much and deserved my lot. Christ, our Saviour, also entered Jerusalem amid the shouts of the people, yet soon He went forth bearing His cross, mocked and derided by that very people. That is my consolation. I am a poor sinner and forgive you gladly." She was then stripped and dressed in the rags of a beggar woman, and in this condition, clutching her wounded child to her breast, was thrown on to a dungcart and conveyed to Heilbronn. We may here mention that her son was brought up to the Church, and she herself ended her days in a Convent.

The sun having now risen, the peasants' camp within the walls of Weinsberg suddenly awoke to a knowledge of what had happened. A general outcry arose against the execution. A council of war was held, but of what actually passed therein little is known. It would seem, however, that at this time a division arose between the leaders. A "moderate" party, to which Metzler and Hipler belonged, definitely formed itself and appears to have got the upper hand. This party wished to give the knight Götz von Berlichingen "with the iron hand" the command of all the insurgent bands. Florian Geyer, on the other hand, seems to have been strongly opposed to this step, though whether he was prepared to pursue the policy of Jäcklein Rohrbach or approved of his recent action it is not easy to say. Certain is it that, from this moment, he and his "black troop" severed themselves from Metzler, Hipler and the "United Contingent," and returned into the Franconian country. The action of Rohrbach may well have had more behind it than the mere thirst for vengeance, however great the part this motive may have played therein. Rohrbach was an extremist who wished to carry the revolution through to its uttermost end. Respecting this end, his ideas may have been somewhat vague, but there is no doubt that he conceived it as involving the total destruction of the feudal orders, as against any mere partial concessions on their part. He may well, therefore, have wished to force the hand of the peasant council by making them feel that they had "burnt their boats". And, certainly, nothing was more calculated to incense the nobles and cut off the possibility of any compromise being arrived at than his "blood-vengeance" on their order at Weinsberg. As a matter of fact, the immediate effect on the authorities was that of a demoralising terror. The Counts Hohenlohe did not hesitate any longer, but immediately sent the two pieces of ordnance and the ammunition which the "United Contingent" had demanded.

Leaving a detachment in Weinsberg, the latter proceeded to Heilbronn, which city they regarded as already as good as won. They were accompanied by two prisoners, the Counts of Löwenstein, clad in peasant's costume, and bearing white staves in their hands, looking, a contemporary notice states, "as frightened as if they were dead". The events at Weisberg had naturally not heel without their affect at Heilbronn. The power of the aristocratic burgher party was completely broken, and the peasants' army entered the gates, after a short parley, almost without resistance. The city council took the oath of allegiance to the "Evangelical Brotherhood," or the "Christian Peasants League" as it was variously termed, and expressed their willingness to negotiate measures with the insurgents and to act as intermediaries towards an understanding with the feudal powers.

Hans Flux, a wealthy baker, a brother-in-law of George Metzler, was the chief go-between in the negotiations. He belonged distinctly to the moderate party, and he found it not difficult to persuade the "United Contingent" to adopt a conciliatory attitude, if only to show their innocence of the Weinsberg affair. It was thus that the understanding was arrived at, the city council promising to pay a subsidy and to furnish 500 men to the peasant army. The "Twelve Articles" were, as a matter of course, to be sworn to. Furthermore, it was agreed that the town should be given into the hands of the peasants on the condition that no house should plundered, save that of the Teutonic knights. The patricians of the town council, who had no intention of keeping their oath where it was possible to break it, no sooner concluded the bargain than they refused to furnish the force promised. Hans Flux, however, who had been the medium of the negotiations, armed the men at his own expense. The situation generally displeased a number of the peasant army. Cries of treachery against Flux began to be heard, especially when it leaked out that he was negotiating with Hipler and Metzler for a modification of the "Twelve Articles". The "black Hoffmann" made an attempt one night to assassinate Flux, as he rode from the peasant camp back into the city, but his horse saved him.

An uncertain tradition relates that the last deed of this extraordinary female was the murder of the crier who proclaimed the annulling of the "Twelve Articles " at Bockingen, a month later, after the reaction had gained the day there. Respecting her death nothing definite is known.

According to the terms of the agreement entered into, the Carmelite monastery was to pay a ransom of 3,000 gulden and the Clara convent 5,000 gulden. Other smaller religious houses were to furnish sums in proportion. The great establishment of the "knights of the Teutonic Order" was reserved for plunder. The heads of the order and most of the inmates made good their escape. In Heilbronn, as in other towns, the wealthy Teutonic heights were a special object of the hatred of the "common man". The ferment among the poor citizens, town proletarians and impoverished guildsmen, was immense, as may be imagined. They had long held secret converse with the peasants and now openly fraternised with them.(2)

The sacking of the wealthy establishment of the knights took place under the aegis of the city council, who sent to see that the place was not set on fire and that the plundering did not extend beyond its precincts. A motley crew of peasants, consisting largely of tenants of the lands belonging to the order, entered the house, armed with weapons of destruction. All documents were torn up and thrown into the moat. Wine, silver and furniture of all sorts were dragged out into the courtyard and sold at an extemporised auction, over which Jäcklein Rohrbach presided. Women carried away acolytes' garments and priests' vestments, and cut them up for clothes for themselves and their children. As soon as the business of plunder and the sale of the booty was duly ended, a feast was spread in the refectory of the house, at which those few of the knights of the order who had remained were compelled to stand and serve with their hats in their hands.

One peasant, who was sitting at table, remarked to a knight standing behind him, "How now, noble sir? To-day, we are the masters of the Teutonic Order," at the same time giving him a hack-handed blow on the paunch, which caused him to stagger back against the wall with a cry. In addition to the furniture, a considerable sum of money was found in the house, of which the tenants of the order claimed the larger share, as having contributed most to the foods. As a matter of fact, a rich booty, sufficient for all, was obtained.

One citizen alone who had been active in the undertaking carried off v chest containing 1,400 gulden to his house.

Meanwhile, the negotiations of the moderate party, which centred in the handing over of the command of the "United Contingent" to Fritz von Berlichingen, went on apace. Götz, the hero of Goethe's well-known drama, who was noted for his artificial iron hand (he having lost his own hand in battle), had been a zealous partisan of the knights' revolt under Sickingen. His deeds as a warrior generally were famous, and he was animated by a special hostility to the clerical order. But, unlike Florian Geyer, he had no real sympathy with the peasants, for whom at heart he entertained much the same feelings as any other noble. Götz had recently appealed to the Franconian knighthood to form a league against the priesthood, and he may have seen in the peasant revolt a possible shoeing-horn to his plans. His immediate reasons, however, for connecting himself with the movement were undoubtedly partly compulsion and partly fear. Nearly all his knightly colleagues had, from dread of the "common man," entered the service of the Swabian League. Götz also offered his services to the league before suffering himself to be nominated to the commandership on the other side. According to his own account, which he gives in his autobiography, it was only through a misunderstanding that this came to pass at all. It is true that his statements require to be taken with some reserve, since the desire, for obvious reasons, to dissociate himself from any sympathy with the peasants and their lost cause is only too apparent throughout the aforesaid work, which, so far as this episode is concerned, is couched in an apologetic tone. It is probable notwithstanding, from all we know of the man, that the account he gives is substantially true. On finding his appeal to the Franconian knighthood unsuccessful, he had, it appears, offered his services to the Count Palatine, his feudal superior. Immediately after the capture of Weinsberg, Götz alleges that he took steps to save his property and family archives, by having them deposited in a town for safety. As, however, no town would accept the responsibility in the event of its being sacked, he abandoned his plan. At the same time he sent a messenger to the "United Contingent" to know what he was to expect. The chief men, as we have seen, were already discussing among themselves the question of offering him the leadership. Finding his messenger's return delayed, he communicated with the marshal of the Count Palatine, Wilhelm von Habern, asking him to protect his castle. Götz's wife, however, and her sister seem to have mistrusted the strength of the authorities to cope with the insurrection. Everywhere around them they saw castles and monasteries falling into the hands of the peasants, so when a letter arrived from the Count Palatine himself, gladly accepting Götz's offer of service and promising the desired protection, the two women concealed the letter and carefully kept the fact of its arrival from the knight's knowledge. In fact, according to Götz's own account, his wife categorically denied having received any reply from the count. "Thereupon" he writes, "I feared me much in that I know not how I should hold myself, the more so in that the story went that the count would make a compact with the peasants."

The upshot was, according to Götz, that, thinking the proposals he had made to the marshal were rejected by the count and fearing for the safety of himself and his castle, he had, like so many other nobles, consented to join the "Evangelical Brotherhood," and was subsequently compelled to take over its command. This was effected almost entirely by the leaders Hipler, Metzler, Berlin (a member by the Heilbronn Council, Flux, and one or two others, amid strong protests from the bulk of the rank and file. With Götz himself, it was a case of Aut Caesar, aut nullus. Non-acceptance, he felt, meant his ruin. The pact between Götz and the peasant leaders was signed and sealed in an inn in the village of Gundelsheim, whither the contingent had retired after leaving Heilbronn. Götz narrates in his autobiography how he rode from one company of the peasant army to another, offering to negotiate peace with the authorities, until he came to that consisting of the tenants of the Counts Hohenlohe. "Here I beheld myself," he says, "suddenly encompassed with muskets, spears, and halberds, pointed at me. They cried that I should be their captain, in whether I would or no. They compelled me to be their fool and leader, and to the end that I might save my body and my life, I must forsooth do as they willed."

Had Götz been sincere in taking up the cause of the rebellion, there is no doubt that, experienced warrior as he was, he would have been a valuable acquisition. Even as it was, some of his suggestions respecting the maintenance of discipline were in the right direction, but the fact remained that he was acting under compulsion in a cause with which he had no sympathy, and that his one concern was to get rid of his responsibility at the first possible moment, if not actually to betray his trust.

The appointment of Götz von Berlichingen was a victory for the moderate party, which had suddenly acquired prominence owing to the action of Rohrbach and his followers at Weinsberg. In addition to this, George Metzler, the trusted leader of the "United Contingent," had been influenced in the direction of moderation by the machinations of his wife, as it would seem, and by the persuasions of her brother, the wealthy master-baker of Heilbronn. There is, however, no reason to think that Metzler was actually a traitor or consciously moved to the course he took by unworthy motives.

The result soon showed itself in a modification of the "Twelve Articles". On this Gotz insisted.

With Hans Berlin and Wendel Hipler, and possibly others, the matter was discussed in a sort of committee. Certain of the "Articles" were declared suspended until the imperial reform which Weigand, Hipler and the Heilbronn permanent committee were sketching out for the consideration of a general congress should be decided upon. Most of the old feudal rights and dues were to be provisionally upheld. There was to be no more plundering. Obedience was provisionally to be paid to constituted authorities, and no new insurrectionary hands were to be formed, in short, with few exceptions, everything was to remain in statu quo until the adoption or introduction of the aforesaid imperial reform.

These modifications were carried by a narrow majority in the council of the "United Contingent." but naturally not without fresh murmuring among the rank and file. Jäcklein Rohrbach and his company had separated at once from the main body on the first symptoms of the new turn that things were taking. Other sections followed later, and the "United Contingent" of the Evangelical Peasant Brotherhood began to acquire an unenviable reputation throughout the movement for "trimming". Certain practical proposals respecting military reorganisation which Hipler at this time put forward, notably the very sensible one to enrol free-lances in the service of the contingent, were incontinently rejected by the peasants, partly from mistrust and partly from an unwillingness to divide the spoil with these experienced booty-hunters. For it must not be supposed that the "United Contingent" observed the rules laid down by Götz and his moderate colleagues anent plundering. They burnt and plundered as much as ever. In fact, in one case only Götz remonstrating with his supposed followers (over whom his actual authority was the very smallest) for destroying a castle which he had given express orders should be spared, he narrowly escaped with his life. He was only saved, indeed, by the prompt appearance of his henchmen, Berlin and Hipler.

On the other hand, however anxious he might be to protect the property of his own immediate order, when the possessions of the Church, which he hated perhaps more than the peasants themselves, were in question, he was perfectly willing to let the contingent have its way to the full. Thus, on the 30th of April, the various bodies comprising the contingent, with Götz and Metzler at their head, appeared before the Benedictine Abbey of Amorbach, in order, as they declared, "as Christian brethren to make a reformation". The inmates were summoned to surrender all their money and treasures on pain of death. But while the negotiations were going on, a body of peasants burst into the house, and the same scene took place as had been enacted in scores of other ecclesiastical buildings for more than a month past. Vestments, chalices, books richly bound, with silver, gold and precious stones, furniture, the contents of the cellars and the granaries, the cattle, in short, all things that were of any value were dragged out and divided amongst the assailants, or destroyed. Götz himself took his share, including the costly vestments of the abbot, who had to go away in a smock which one of the peasants had given him out of compassion. The immediate plan of operations was to proceed to the assistance of the insurgents in the Archbishopric of Mainz and the Bishopric of Würzburg, and then by way of Frankfurt to invade the Archbishoprics of Trier and of Cologne. It was a favourite scheme of Götz to divide up ecclesiastical property amongst the knightly order. Hipler and Metzler may well have been persuaded that leniency towards the lower nobilty and its possessions, combined with the prospect of obtaining a share of those of the Church, would induce the former, if not to actively support the peasants cause, at least to waver in their fidelity to the imperial authorities.

In Mainz, the cardinal-archbishop was seriously considering the question of secularising his territories, and had been, in fact, in correspondence with Luther on the subject, a plan which he abandoned, owing, it is said, to the influence of his mistress. On the approach of the peasants, the envoys, not of the archbishop, who had fled, but of the Bishop of Strasburg, whom he had left in charge of his affairs, hastened to sign the modified "Twelve Articles," and to pay a ransom of 15,000 golden. In the whole territory of the archbishopric, including the towns of Mainz and Aschaffenburg, the insurrection was now in full swing.

It had even reached the neighbouring free imperial city of Frankfurt-on-the-Main, where the leaders of the city-proletariat had extorted from the council a charter of rights and privileges containing forty-five "articles ". An insurrectionary committee, mainly composed of small craftsmen, under the leadership of a shoemaker, had been formed in the town and was in perpetual session, having relations with the peasants of the surrounding territories and with the small towns of the neighbourhood.

The "United Contingent," under Götz and Metzler, after reducing Aschaffenburg to submission, now decided to make straight for Würzburg, where the main body of the Franconian insurgents was encamped, their efforts being directed towards the capture of the important fortress on the Frauenberg which commanded the city.

Amongst the free imperial towns now threatened by the insurrection, none were more hardly pressed than Schwabisch Hall, lying on the borderland between Swabia and Franconia. Like other imperial cities, Hall had an extensive territory outside its walls, cultivated by a numerous peasantry, to which it and its council stood in the feudal relation of overlord. The peasants of this countryside and of those adjoining it had risen in the usual way. They formed themselves into companies with leaders, and arranged a plan of campaign for capturing the city, but it seems that these particular peasants were exceptionally well-to-do and accustomed to good living, and their fighting capacity seems to have been in inverse proportion to their boon companionship. They possessed, indeed, muskets and ordnance, but as a general rule they contented themselves with the ordinary dagger as their weapon. Instead of making straight for their objective, this contingent, which was over 3,000 strong "turned in" at every village on the way, making free with the wine-cellars of the priests, the Bürgermeisters and the monks, whom they compelled to carouse with them. When, finally, they came within striking distance of the city, all they could do was to encamp and fall asleep. The town of Hall was, of course, in trepidation, having, like the rest, within its walls its own discontented population, which was well disposed to the cause of the peasants, and the authorities were not in a position to withstand the force of the movement from within and from without. Some of the country people had made so sure of getting into possession of the town that they had actually fixed upon the houses they were going to appropriate. The well-beliquored peasants were, however, awakened at break of day by a shot from the neighbouring height. This was followed by a second and a third. The peasant camp was in confusion. Many in their still bibulous condition believed themselves struck and fell down accordingly, The rest scattered precipitately. The fact was that a small party had started from the town to reconnoitre, bringing with them a few hand-guns, but, as it happened, without shot. Seeing the state of affairs in the camp below them, they had fired more in jest than for any other reason. The upshot was that the peasants of the imperial city of Hall were glad to be allowed to return to their homesteads on renewing their oath of fidelity to the city, and thus the rebellion of the Hall peasants ignominiously collapsed.

The movement in Würtemberg, meanwhile, went on apace; but it was moderated by the influence of Matern Feuerbatcher, the well-to-do innkeeper of Bottwar, who was anxious to remain on good terms with all sides, and, as we have seen, only placed himself at the head of the peasant force under compulsion and to a certain extent with the consent of some of his noble patrons. On their advice, he made it a special stipulation that he would have nothing to do with the "Weinsbergers," understanding thereby the party of Jäcklein Rohrbach, who had been the agents in the slaughter of the knights. In Stuttgart the excitement was so great that the members of the regency, representing the Austrian Government, had fled, together with some of the patrician members of the city council. The chief pastor of the city, Dr. Johannes Mantel, was a zealous patron of the new doctrines, for which he had suffered imprisonment, being liberated by the peasants. After some negotiations, the peasants were admitted into the town, but they only remained within the walls for two days. The ransom money- exacted for religious establishments and from the town itself was comparatively moderate. After two days, the contingent left the city for the Valley of the Rems, in order to drive back an extraneous body of peasants, who were now accused of plundering; for Matern Feuerbacher and the other leaders of the Würtemberg movement had pledged themselves not to allow foreign elements to intrude into the duchy. Here, as elsewhere, the Weinsberg affairs had strongly influenced the trend of sentiment, both within and without the movement, within by strengthening moderate counsels, and without by first of all terrorising and afterwards exacerbating the princes and nobles against the peasants and their demands. It is only one instance of the policy pursued by all governing classes in exploiting the conscience of mankind. Of the causes of the insurrection itself, of the infamous oppression of the feudal orders, no notice, of course, is taken. Of the slaughter by knights, well-armed and equipped, and experienced in the fighting art, of unarmed or badly-armed peasants, sometimes even of country-folk who were not in rebellion, of the atrocities of this nature committed by that very Helferstein, whose death was only the just penalty of his crimes, similarly nothing is said. Hundreds of peasants foully massacred count for nothing; the important event, the "great crime." calculated to produce in all men a "thrill of horror," is that eighteen knights, the authors and abettors of these things, are slain by an act of justice, or, if you will, vengeance.

It was the same in the contest between the workmen of Paris and the reactionaries of Versailles, in the spring of 1871. The governing classes and all those who took their cue from them (either through interested motives, want of knowledge of the facts, or indifference), were, or pretended to be, dissolved in horror at the execution of seventy-two persons belonging to these classes. They had not one word to say in condemnation of the systematic butchery one or two months previously in cold blood of insurgent prisoners of war, culminating perhaps in the vastest massacre on record, by the authorities representing those governing classes. Yet it was this that led up to the act of vengeance against which they pretend such an overflowing indignation.

Once more, the torturing and doing to death of nine working men, after a mock trial, by order of the late Spanish Minister, Canovas, is a trifle; but no sooner is their death avenged on Canovas himself by a self-sacrificing fanatic than the governing classes and their organs talk with duly impressive fervour of the "sanctity of human life" and of the exceeding infamy of violating it. The power of position and wealth to create a public conscience agreeable to its interests, and to suit its purposes, is indeed convenient and wonderful.

The German peasants of 1525, as did the Commune of Paris, and as is the wont of successful insurgents generally, signalised their success as a rule by their studied moderation and good-nature, as contrasted with the ferocious cruelty of their enemies, the constituted authorities.

Notes

1. Landesknechte or lanzknechte I shall in future throughout this work translate by its nearest English equivalent — free-lances.

2. On the poverty of some of the proletarians of Heilbronn, an inventory subsequently taken throws some light. The possessions of one were found to be limited to a bed, an old wooden bedstead and two pillows, on which six children were lying. Another with four children had only a table and a small bed. A third, also with four children, could only boast an old bedstead, a can, and a piece of armour.

Chapter V. The Peasants War in Franconia

THE starting point and centre of the insurrectionary movement in the Franconian districts of middle Germany was the free imperial city of Rothenburg-on-the-Tauber, a town situated on a plateau of table-land in the valley watered by the little river Tauber (cf. German Society, pp. 208. 209). As we have before seen, the rival of Martin Luther, Andreas Bodenstein, better known as Dr. Karlstadt, betook himself here, after having been compelled to leave Wittenberg. Another preacher, Joahann Deuschlin, had already discoursed on the new doctrines in the town for a year or two previously. Deuschlin's career, like his doctrines, bore a striking resemblance to that of Hubmeyer. He also had undertaken an anti-Jewish campaign and had been instrumental in the destruction of Jewish quarters and synagogues before his conversion to the new revolutionary principles, political and religions. One of his most zealous disciples and co-operators was Hans Schmidt, a blind monk. The Teutonic Order in Rothenburg, as in other towns, possessed an establishment, but in this case the preacher Deuschlin succeeded in gaining over certain of their number to the Reformation, and indeed Melchior, one of the heads of the order, had even ventured to marry publicly with the usual festivities, and as fate had it, to marry the sister of Hans Schmidt, the blind monk. The two preachers had severely, attacked the Commenthur, or supreme head of the order, and had so far carried their point as to get him deposed and another Commenthur, Christen, established in his place. These things, of course, did not go on without friction with the Episcopal authorities at Würzburg. but for the moment the revolutionary party remained victorious.

By the end of March, the peasant population in the territory belonging to Rothenburg had begun to assemble with a view to revolutionary action, whilst inside the town the ex-Bürgermeister, Ehrenfried Kumpf, the Church reformer, had inaugurated an iconoclastic campaign, in the course of which priests and choristers were driven from the cathedral, the mass-book was hurled from the altar, images and pictures were mutilated and destroyed, and the chapel of the immaculate virgin was levelled with the ground. Karlstadt followed in the same strain. A richly ornamented and endowed church, just outside the walls, was plundered by the members of the miller's guild, and costly pictures, images and plate were thrown into the Tauber. But while Kumpf remained a mere anti-popish fanatic, Karlstadt went forward on the lines of the political movement. The party of the people within the walls had now become strong mop, as usual, sympathised with the peasants without. The latter, on the 6th of March, presented their grievances to the city council in the form of "articles," which in this, as in so many other cases, had been drawn up by ex-priests. The part that the recalcitrant clergy played in the political and social, no less than the religious movement of the time, we have more than once had occasion to remark. These "articles" were of the usual character, alleging the weight of feudal dues — many of them of recent imposition. The appeal to the religious sentiment in them is also strong. The negotiations, however, which ensued did not result in any definite agreement.

Karlstadt, who had fled from Orlamunde to Rothenburg, was received on his arrival with acclamation by the town populace. The Markgraf Casimir set a price upon his heed, but Karlstadt, notwithstanding that, once within the walls of Rothenburg, felt himself comparatively secure and did not hesitate to preach openly even in the streets. The inner council, manned as usual by the patrician class, eventually forbade him the right of preaching and at the same time withdrew from him permission to reside in the town. The council in this matter, there is no doubt, acted partly in obedience to strong pressure from outside. In consequence, the learned agitator found it necessary to disappear for a time. It was given out by his friends that he had repaired to Strassburg. The truth was that he was in hiding within the city in the houses of the preacher Deuschlin, the new Commenthur of the Teutonic Order, Christen, the ex-Bürgermeister and iconoclast Kumpf, and especially in that of the master-tailor Phillip. During his concealment and supposed absence, tracts and brochures from the peal of Karlstadt found a mysterious circulation in the town, his friends having seen to the printing of them, whilst there were plenty of willing hands to attend to their sale or distribution.

One of the most active leaders in the revolt was Stephan Menzingen, a Swabian knight of an old family and a partisan of Duke Ulrich, who had married the daughter of one of the city councillors and had been admitted to the citizenship. From this, in consequence of a quarrel with the council on a question of taxation, he had subsequently withdrawn, and had taken up his abode in northern Switzerland, whence he suddenly returned to Rothenburg early in the year 1525, in time to take part in the new religious and political movement. He was instrumental in procuring the formation of it citizen's committee, to which all prominent members of the people's party belonged and which served as a sort of counterpoise to the aristocratic council. It was this committee that brought the peasants' demands before the council. By the end of March, Menzingen had carried the matter so far that the great council of the town dissolved itself, many of its members joining the new citizens committee, which now formally constituted itself the governing power of the town, while the small or executive council was allowed to continue on its good behaviour, after having sworn to carry out the will of the citizens or to abdicate. The victory was now practically won for the new gospel of "evangelical brotherly love," according to which all things should be in common, and the authority of status should cease. As reported by a contemporary writer, "the common people did will that one should have as much as another and no more, that it should be the duty of one to lend to another, but that none should require of another that he should give back and repay" (Thomas Zweifel ap. Baumann, Quellen aus Rothenburg). The alliance with the peasants, the tenants of the city lands without the gates, was now concluded.

Karlstadt now came out of his hiding-place, Kumpf openly admitting that he had given him shelter. On being remonstrated with by his old colleagues of the council, Kumpf replied that he had acted in the service of God and for the food of the town, always believing Karlstadt to be the man to negotiate between the town and the peasants. No little wonder, as may be imagined, was excited by the sudden reappearance of a man believed to be at the time in another part of Germany. The Rothenberg peasants now began to adopt the some tactic, as those of other parts. Whoever refused to join their "brotherhood" had his house sacked, if not also burnt down. A "high time" moreover was had with clerical winecellars, whilst in the town itself the clergy were compelled to supply gratuitously the poorer citizens, who quartered themselves upon them. The peasant army already numbered from four to five thousand men, and the leaders, amongst whom were some impoverished knights, better understood the art of war and military organisation than those of some of the other contingents.

A part of their force remained encamped near the town, while the rest swept along the valley of the Tauber. Chief among the military heads of the Franconian peasant forces was the knight Florian Geyer, to whom we had occasion to refer in the last chapters Little is known of his antecedents, save that he was the lord of the old castle of Giebelstadt, near Würzburg. He suddenly appeared on the scene in the Tauber valley at the end of March, 1525, with a small company of free-lances that he had engaged, and shortly after he took over the command of the Rothenberg Landwehr, a body whose members were enrolled for the defence of the Rothenberg territory, on the initiation of the revolution. But of these two elements he formed his famous "Black Troop," a company distinguished among the peasant force; for its bravery, cohesion and organisation. Florian Geyer, though himself a noble, threw himself heart and soul into the peasant cause, championing the most radical demands of the popular party, notably advising the destruction of all castles, and the reduction of their lords to the status of simple citizens or tillers of the soil. The fame of his "Black Troop" soon spread far and wide, and its co-operation was eagerly sought by other bands.

The Franconian insurrection had now spread to the immediate territory of the Bishop of Würzburg. Early in April, the whole diocese was in motion, in the towns no less than in the countryside. On the 5th of the month, Fritz Lobel, another Franconian knight, led a body of peasants to the sack of the wealthy Carthusian monastery of Zächelhausen. The chapter at Würzburg became alarmed, and sent three canons to secure the allegiance, amid the general collapse of authority, of the town of Ochsenfurt, but they were received with closed gates and had to remain outside all night. Eventually, the town consented to a pact with the Episcopal authorities on the basis of certain substantial concessions, which the latter were compelled with a heavy heart to grant by charter.

In the Würzburg territories the insurrection was carried on largely through an association founded here again by two preachers, and bearing the name of the "infinites" or "eternals" ("Die Unendlichen"). One township after another was won. Everywhere the alarm-bell clanged forth, calling to arms all within the walls. In the north of the diocese, the drum of insurrection first made itself heard on the 9th of April. The matter followed its usual course. In a few days the original small band had increased to formidable dimensions and had been joined by other bands. Monasteries of various orders were entered and plundered. Within the walls of the townships, as usual, the Teutonic Order fared worst of all.

The bishop of Wiirzberg and Duke of Franconia, Konrad von Thungen became now seriously alarmed, especially on hearing that the peasants of the Rothenberg Landwehr led by Florian Geyer, meditated making a descent upon Würzburg. In vain he sought help from the surrounding districts. In vain he applied to the Bishop of Romberg, whose hands were full with his own rebellious subjects: in vain to the Swabian League, which offered to pay for three hundred horsemen for a month, if they could be obtained, but sent neither man nor horse. The duke-bishop assembled his vassals, his "noble counsellors," to consult what measures should be adopted. Opinions were divided. Some thought that active steps should be taken against the recalcitrant country people, and that the wives and children of those who had banded themselves together should he driven from their homesteads and villages, and the latter set on lire. Others feared to take immediate repressive measures, more especially as the neighbouring princes had hitherto held their hands, arguing the meagreness of the bishop's resources and contending for a policy of delay until an arrangement could be come to with the adjacent potentates. This view was finally adopted. The peasants, as a result, pursued their course unopposed. "Where they came, or where they lay," writes Lorenz Fries, the Prince-Bishop's Private Secretary, "they fell upon the monasteries, the priests' houses, the chests and the cellars of the authority, consuming in gluttony and in drunkenness that which they found. And it did exceedingly please this new brotherhood that they might consume by devouring and drinking their fill, and had not had to pay withal. More drunken, more full-bellied, more helpless folk, one had hardly seen together than during the time of this rebellion. So that I know not whether the peasants' device and conduct, had they but abstained from fire and bloodshed, should rather be called a carnival's jest or a war .. . and whether a peasants war, and not rather a wine-war"

So much from a hostile source. It must, however, be admitted by the best friends of the peasants and their cause that gluttony and wine-bibbing contributed as potently as any other influence to the politically unproductive character of the peasant successes and to that lack of cohesion and discipline which led the way to the final catastrophe and soaked the German soil with the blood of its tillers.

All authority throughout the bishopric of Würzburg was now paralysed. Even the Count Hennenberg, whose, territory lay on its northern frontier, the most powerful feudatory cf the bishop, showed no sign of furnishing his overlord with men or money, but, on the contrary as it soon appeared, was entering into negotiations with a view to adoption into the "Christian Brotherhood" — an event which shortly after happened. The count was required, at the same time, to furnish his tenants with a charter of emancipation and to swear to act in accordance with the Word of God and with the precepts of the Gospel.

Würzburg itself, the seat of government and residence of the bishop and his chapter, soon showed signs of disaffection. The town had been captured a century before by the then duke-bishop by force of arms, and deprived of its ancient municipal rights. This had never been forgotten. So, one fine day, a body of the poorer citizens were to be seen gathered together in an earnest discussion near the gate of St. Stephen. A prebendary of the cathedral, who was passing by at the time, and who fancied he heard himself unfavourably criticised by some of the crowd, began to call them names, and to threaten to have their heads struck off on the market-place. The news of the abuse and the threat flew through the poorer townsfolk like lightning. An uproar was the result, the populace marching with arms and in extemporised battle array to the sound of pipe and drum before the residences of the cathedral authorities. The disturbance was only partially and for the moment quelled by the gift of a tun of wine to the people by one of the canons. In a day or two, affairs had come to such a pass that the bishop betook himself to the overhanging fortress on the Frauenberghill, the Marienburg, as it was called, after having provided the stronghold with victuals to sustain a siege, and having given orders that all available men-at-arms and loyal subjects capable of such service, from the town and country round, should he brought in to garrison the place.

Those among the patrician councillors of the city, who had fled to the stronghold of authority, escaped with their bishop, and, after having conferred with the latter, sent Sebastian von Rotenham and two others of their number down into the town to discuss with the citizens, and to seek by threats or cajolery to bring them to obedience. They were to secure the punishment of the ringleaders and if possible the expulsion of unruly and dangerous elements from within the walls, and further to see that the town was placed in a proper state of defence against peasant lands from outside.

Rotenham and his companions rode pompously through the streets, and, calling together the heads of the different wards, handed over to them his instructions. Thinking to frighten the Würzhurgers, he at the same time announced that a body of horsemen was on its way and had orders to quarter itself in the town. This threat, which Rotenham had no instructions to make, had as its only result to precipitate matters. The leaders of the movement were at once aroused, urging the citizens to close the gates against any force the bishop might send. The citizens, they said, or at least the "common man" of the town — in the language familiar now everywhere to the dwellers within walls, when the man from the open country knocked at their gates — had no cause of quarrel with the peasant, who was his brother. So, far from fighting against him or refusing him admittance, they should both join hands in a common brotherhood against the oppressor, be he prince or prelate, noble or city-magnate. The peasants were only fighting for the Gospel, said they. A dissolute priesthood had already seduced enough burghers' wives and daughters. Would they march out to fight the peasants leaving their women a prey to such? Already it was alleged that ordnance was being placed in position by the bishop's orders to attack the town, should it refuse him obedience.

Excitement manifested itself on all hands. In response to the exhortations of the agitators, towers and gates were soon garrisoned by sturdy burghers. The warden of the fishers' guild saw that the approaches to the river- the Main — were duly secured by heavy chains; he also took in charge defensive operations as regards the paths leading up the Frauenberg. Up these paths Rotenhan and his two colleagues now wended their sorrowful way back to the castle with the tidings that their mission had proved a failure. Further intercourse between the castle and town was now rendered well-nigh impossible by the defensive obstructions alone, apart from the fact that the vintners' guild had organised itself into a company of sharp-shooters, to "pot," from behind the vines which covered the slopes of the Frauenberg, any knight, patrician or prelate, who might be seeking his way to the town from the heights above. The cooks' and the carpenters' guilds alike refused to obey the mandate calling upon them to furnish certain of their number for service in the Marienburg. It fared now badly with the ecclesiastical foundations and residences within the town. Wine-cellars and larders, as may be imagined, were not spared more in Würzburg than elsewhere.

But negotiations were not yet entirely broken off between the bishop and the city. On the 13th of April, a delegation went up to the castle to negotiate, with the result that the bishop was compelled to call a Landtag for the 30th of the month, consisting of representatives of the knighthood and the towns, at which all grievances were to be discussed and considered.

At the same time that these things were passing in Würzburg, the five different bodies of insurgents, which had formed in the northern part of the Duchy of Franconia, united themselves into a single contingent with a commander and military organisation. On the 15th of April, amidst the flames of castles and monasteries fallen an easy prey to the peasant bands, a great council of war was held at which it was decided to at once advance on Würzburg. The negotiations with Count Henneberg, however, which were not concluded till some days later, delayed matters for a time.

On the 2nd of May the bishop with certain of his councillors descended, under a promise of safe conduct, into the town to open the Landtag agreed on. This was against the advice of many of his following, who thought the proceeding dangerous and would have liked the Landtag to have been called on the Frauenberg, or, indeed, anywhere else rather than in the now openly-rebellious town of Würzburg. However, as a large number of representatives had already assembled, no other course seemed possible. Before the proceedings had fairly begun, loud complaints reached the bishop's ears of the oppression of the "common man" by his prelates, contrary to the Word of God, and of how the Word of God, which had only a few years ago been again brought to light, was being smothered and its preachers persecuted. Many of the town representatives demanded that the peasants should be called upon to send their own delegates to confer in the deliberations. With this demand the bishop was, much against his will, compelled to comply. The response, however, was not satisfactory. The peasantry of the Tauber valley answered the bishop's messengers that at the moment it was not the time for deliberating at diets, but that they would reserve anything they had to say till they arrived in force at Würzburg, which would be before long. The same with other districts. All saw now that things had gone too far to be settled in the way proposed. The result was the collapse of the Landtag, which was hastily closed, every man riding away to his own town or castle.

There was now a formal understanding between the town of Würzburg and the insurgents in the open country. The bishop on his side took his measures, collecting the garrisons, such as they were, from neighbouring castles to reinforce the Frauenberg. The united insurgent contingent from the north was now encamped before the gates, where it was joined in a day or two by Florian Geyer and his black troop from the Tauber valley, and almost immediately after, as before related, by the famous "United Contingent" of George Metzler and Wendel Hipler. In this extremity, the bishop was advised as a last resort, to apply personally to the Elector Palatine for assistance. On the 5th of May, accordingly, with a heavy heart, he rode down, accompanied by a few followers, from the Frauenberg, his last remaining stronghold, into the plain, and struck out westward towards Heidelberg, where he arrived two days later.

The castle of the Marienburg on the Frauenberg was now garrisoned by 244 men-at-arms, besides ecclesiastics, nobles and servants. The Markgraf Friedrich of Brandenburg was left as commander, while Rotenhan undertook the victualling. Florian Geyer and his black troop were soon followed by the whole of the Tauber-valley contingent, which recruited itself, during a victorious march, with hundreds of new followers. The course of the "Franconian Army," as the Tauber-valley contingent now called itself, was characterised, needless to say, by the usual plunder and destruction, an especially rich booty being furnished by the wealthy Cistercian foundation at Ebrich. Flocks and herds were slaughtered or driven away, larders and cellars emptied of their contents, precious stones and gold torn out of the settings; vestments, chalices and ornaments appropriated, and the building finally given over to the flames.

With the advent of the Tauber-valley peasantry on Würzburg there was united, in and around the town, the greatest force of the peasant army at that moment to be found at any one point throughout Germany. Most of the ablest leaders from a military point of view were also present — Metzler, Hipler, not to mention Götz von Berlichingen, and, above all, Florian Geyer. But, as the event turned out, this almost solitary instance of co-operation on a great scale between different sections of the insurgents proved not only a failure in itself, but a source of weakness to the whole movement. The peasants of middle Germany placed too heavy stakes on this one event, the capture of the Frauenberg. Now the Frauenberg itself was a strong natural strategic position, and the Marienburg, the object of attack, was an exceptionally well-built and well-appointed mediaeval fortress. It had been thoroughly victualled, so that it would take some time to reduce by famine, and it was well-garrisoned with experienced fighting-men, with no lack of weapons, ordnance and ammunition. The result was as might have been expected; valuable as the acquisition of the Frauenberg would have been to the peasant cause, yet the chance of capturing it was not worth the price paid. For what was the price? Nothing less than the locking up at one point of a force constituting the main strength of the insurrection — a force comprising the only reliable military nucleus in the whole movement. Had a plan of campaign been worked out, according to which by means of rapid marches this force or portions of it should have undertaken the task of supporting the movement generally at places where it needed support in conjunction with the local insurgent bands, the contest would undoubtedly have been prolonged, and though complete success may not have been possible, owing to the political and economical trend of the time, the completeness of the catastrophe, which nearly everywhere overtook the movement, would almost certainly have been averted.

The peasants, in accordance with the pact made with the town, had free ingress and egress. The sympathetic citizens, of course, fraternised with them, though possibly they may have winced somewhat at the free and easy behaviour of their guests at times and at the outspokenness of the communistic sentiments expressed.

According to a contemporary, the peasants "were always full (drunken); showed much ill-behaviour in word and deed, and neither in the afternoon nor the morning would they be ruled by any". The language was openly heard that, since they were brethren, it was only fair that all things should be equal, and that the rich should divide with the poor, especially they who had acquired their wealth through trade or otherwise gained it from the poor man. The improved discipline sought to be introduced by the leaders of the "United Contingent" proved as impossible to carry out in the camp and in the city as it had been on the march. The orders issued in this sense remained for the most part unobeyed. Even the gallows erected on the market-place proved no adequate deterrent. In fact, in most of the companies, a tendency to insubordination was, as might be expected, increased by the life of idleness and dissipation, which the camp and

Würzburg afforded them. In vain the leaders endeavoured to drive home to their following the fable of the "head and the members". In vain they descanted on the impossibility of a "civil brotherly constitution" without the maintenance of an organised administration. The reply was that they were brothers, and would be equal.

Even after the departure of the bishop, negotiations 'with the Marienburg were not finally broken off. On the 9th of May, the dean of the cathedral with some canons and knights descended into the town, and met the leaders, Götz, Metzler, Geyer, and others, in the inn, whose sign was, the "Green Tree". They pleaded their willingness and that of the bishop to make concessions as regarded the "Twelve Articles". Götz and Metzler seem to have been anxious to accept the terms offered, which included a truce until some of their number could go to and from Heidelberg to obtain the bishop's consent; but Florian Geyer was strongly opposed to any compromise, believing in the possibility of compelling the castle to an unconditional surrender within a few days. When the matter was brought before a general council of the peasants, Florian, with his accustomed fire, observed: "The time is come; the axe is laid to the root of the tree; the dance has now begun, and before the door of every prince shall it be piped. Will we hold back the axe? Will we, of ourselves, turn aside?" Others followed in the same strain, with the result that the terms proposed by the dean and his colleagues were rejected and the siege continued.

A few days later, another attempt at negotiation was made. Götz and Metzler were now more emphatic than ever in their advice to come to terms. Götz reasonably urged the Imprudence of lying idle with their immense force for weeks, awaiting the surrender of the impregnable Frauenberg, and pointed out very justly that there was more important work to do, even going so far as to propose as an alternative an attempt to capture the imperial city of Nürnberg. In this advice, Götz undoubtedly bore himself and his order more in mind than the peasants. In his capacity of knight, he despised and hated the burgher as much as he did the priest. But it was all of no avail. Either from a false view of the situation or, as is more probable, from an unwillingness to exchange the ease and good living afforded them by the bishop's capital for the dangers and hardships of a serious campaign, none of the contingents would consent to abandon the Frauenberg.

On May 14-15, the castle was stormed. With much shouting and beating of drums, several companies, foremost among them the "Black Troop," swarmed up the Frauenberg. The light stockade was swept away, the moat was crossed, the assailants reached to the very walls. But it was only to be received by a rain of bullets, missiles of burning pitch, huge stones from windows and battlements, followed by the thunder of all the ordnance with which the castle was provided. Twice the attacking:, party was driven back with enormous loss. Hundreds of peasants lay dead and dying in, the moats. Seen from the town, the whole castle appeared brilliantly illuminated. It was clear that so long as provisions and powder and shot remained in the castle, the Frauenberg was not to be captured. The idea of taking the fortress by storm before a breach had been made in the walls was in itself chimerical. As ill-luck would have it, moreover, the peasantry's greatest military genius, Florian Geyer, was absent when the storming was decided upon, having gone to Rothenburg to demand ordnance of a larger calibre than any in the peasant camp, and to negotiate for the formal adoption of that town into the "Evangelical Brotherhood". Even Wendel Hipler was not there, having left for Heilbronn to attend the permanent official committee there sitting, to elaborate, in conjunction with Friedrich Weigand and the rest, the scheme of imperial reform already spoken of. Discouraged at the result of their unsuccessful attempts at taking the fortress by storm, the peasants continued the siege in the hope of starving it into surrender. But this took longer than they imagined.

Meanwhile, the popular cause scored another success by the formal entry of the city of Rothenburg into the "Evangelical Brotherhood". On the appeal of the peasant-contingents being handed in to the council by Florian Geyer and his colleagues, the whole body of the poorer citizens threatened to march out with all the ordnance and join the peasants against the town if a favourable response were not given. Even the free-lances in the service of the city threatened to desert to the enemy as soon as it should appear before the gates. The fortunes of Rothenburg were now completely in the hands of the populace. A resolution had been carried for the communisation of ecclesiastical goods. The stores of corn and wine were also to be divided in equal shares between the citizens. Jewels and chalices were to be sold, and with the proceeds of the sale the citizens were to be armed and maintained. A fine frolic went on within the walls. According to contemporary accounts, "old and young did drink and became drunken. Many lay in the streets who could go no further, especially young children who had made them selves overfull with wine."

Rothenburg formally entered the "Evangelical Brotherhood" on the 14th of May, under the following pledges: Firstly, shall the general assembly of burghers set up the Evangelical doctrine, the Holy Word of God, and shall see that the same be preached in pure simplicity without superaddition of human teaching. And what the Holy Gospel doth set up, shall be set up; what it layeth low, shall be laid low, and shall so remain. And, in the meanwhile, no interest due or aught such thing shall be given to any lord until by those most learned in the Holy, Divine, and true Scripture shall a Reformation have been appointed. Injurious castles, water-houses and fortresses, whence hitherto a dreadful oppression have been practised upon the "common man," shall be broken up or consumed by fire. Yet what is therein of goods that can be borne shall go to them who would be brethren, and who have committed naught against the general assembly. Such ordnance as may be found in these houses shall belong to the general assembly. Clergy and lay-men, nobles and commons, shall henceforth hold to the right of the plain citizen and the peasant, and shall be no more than the "common man ". The nobles shall surrender to the assembly all goods of clergy or others, especially of them of their own class, who have done aught against the brotherhood, on pain of loss of life and goods. And, in fine, every man, be he church-man or lay-man, shall henceforth hold in all obedience that which is ordained in the reformation and order concluded by them who are learned in the Holy Scripture.

The city thus entered the "Evangelical Brotherhood" for the formal term of 101 years. The best and heaviest pieces of ordnance in its possession were, with the requisite powder and balls, handed over to the peasants. The late Bürgermeister, Ehrenfried Kumpf, the zealous church-reformer and iconoclast, clad in full armour, rode back with the peasant delegates to the camp of Würzburg. Six hundred Rothenburg peasants, fully armed and equipped, followed with the two guns and the powder-waggon. By the aid of the new artillery, the assailants succeeded in making some impression on the walls of the Marienburg, but, even now, no serious damage appears to have been done. News now came of the successful advance of Truchsess and the army of the Swabian League in the south. The leaders all saw the urgent necessity of making an end of this Würzburg business at the earliest possible date. On the 20th of May, they, through a public crier, offered the entire booty to be found in the castle, including gold, silver, jewels and furniture, together with the assurance of a high rate of continuous pay to any company that should first carry the castle by storm. They, indeed, endeavoured to form a special company for the purpose, keeping a list of volunteers before them in the "Green Tree," where they sat as an executive council; but it all came to nothing.

In the neighbouring Bishopric of Bamberg, the insurrection had also broken out about the same time as in the Würzburg territories. The chief preacher of the new doctrines here was one Johann Schwanhäuser. Like his colleagues elsewhere, he attacked in the first instance the clergy and then proceeded to descant on general social inequalities. The clergy were hypocrites and godless men, "they do thrust Christ out of the vineyard," said Schwanhäuser, "and do set up themselves in His stead. They call themselves the vicegerents of Christ, and the true ambassadors are persecuted by them. They let the poor sit without houses, perish with cold and starve, yet to dead saints do they build great stone houses and bear to them gold, silver and precious stones. Were we true Christians," he added, "we should sell monstrances, chalices, church and mass vestments, and live as the twelve apostles, giving all our surplusage to the poor."

The sermons of Schwanhäuser worked in Bamberg, as similar discourses had worked elsewhere, like a spark, firing the inflammable material furnished in such quantity both within and without walls at this epoch. On the 11th of April, the tocsin rang out from the belfry of the town, and Bamberg proclaimed itself in insurrection. The town populace formed itself into companies, chose leaders, closed the gates, and compelled members of the town patriciate and the clergy to assist. They sent messengers throughout all the country round, urging the villages to join them. On the bishop's refusal to surrender the church property, his castle above the town, which was practically undefended, was taken by assault, pillaged and burnt. For three days the usual scenes of plunder took place in and around Bamberg.

On the 15th of April, however, a compromise was arrived at with the bishop, by which he was recognised as the sole responsible authority in the land, the chapter losing all its separate rights. The bishop on his side promised to call a Landtag for the discussion and removal of all grievances. This treaty, although publicly proclaimed in the streets, does not seem to have been of much effect. The destruction of castles and monasteries throughout the episcopal territories went on apace. As many as seventy castles, besides religious houses, fell a prey to rapine and flames. Crowds from the country-side flocked into the capital. An old chronicle informs us that "no one was certain of his life and goods, after the multitude had bedrunk themselves in the wine-cellars of the churchmen, as continually came to pass. So evil and so unruly did it become in Bamberg, that not alone the old pious burghers were grieved thereat, but also the others, even they who had, at first, had right good pleasure in the tumult."

By the middle of April the movement was everywhere reaching its height, and was not to be quelled by promises or even by written concessions any more than by threats. The insurrection was going from one success to another.

Chapter VI. The Movement in the East and West

WE have now to follow the rise and progress of the movement in the eastern Austrian territories of Tyrol and Salzburg. We shall then briefly trace its fortunes in the western dependencies of Austria, in the Breisgau and Upper Elsass, and along the Rhine.

In the first rank of the prince-ecclesiastics of the extensive hereditary domains of the house of Austria stood the Archbishop of Salzburg. Amongst the numerous well-hated prince-prelates of the age, Archbishop Matthaus Lang by no means took a back place. The town of Salzburg had long been at cross purposes with the arch-episcopal castle overhanging it. History tells how the predecessor of Lang, Leonhard by name, had invited the bürgermeister and some distinguished members of the city-council to a banquet. As soon as they sat down to table, he caused the castle banqueting-hall to fill with armed men, to whom he gave orders for his guests to be seized, fettered and carried off to a distant portion of his territories to be executed. The reason of this act of treachery was a report that had reached his ears of the intention of the council to apply to the emperor for a charter constituting Salzburg a free city. This act, however, seems to have excited less indignation amongst the body of the burghers, owing to the class hatred entertained for the wealthy town patricians whom it immediately concerned.

As for the peasants in the Salzburg lands, they, like other peasantries on ecclesiastical domains, had a standing quarrel with their lord, and had more than once risen against what, they deemed unjust exactions during the latter half of the preceding century. It was natural, therefore, that the great popular wave of 1525 should not have passed over the town and country of Salzburg without leaving its impression.

The then Archbishop Matthaus Lang came to his see in 1519. He had sprung from a patrician family of the town of Augsburg, and by cunning and diplomacy had attained to one of the wealthiest and most powerful sees in the empire. His character may be judged from the statement of one of his own privy councillors that "it were well known with what roguery and knavery he had come into the benefice, how his whole life long he had naught that was good in his thought, was full of malice, a knave, and his disposition never good towards his countryfolk". That the foregoing estimate is in nowise too severe his public acts amply testify.

On the opening of the Lutheran Reformation, it is not surprising that the Salzburgers showed themselves eminently favourable to the new doctrines. Here, as elsewhere, were to be found enthusiastic reformers amongst the clergy. With these must be included the confessor of the archbishop himself. No sooner did the latter become aware of the fact than he threw the priest, whose name was Kastenbauer, into prison, and gave orders for all those acknowledging the Lutheran heresy, were they clerical or lay, to be pursued with heavy pains and penalties. But the cunning prelate had a plan in view for making the spread of the Lutheran movement a shoeing-horn to an ambitious scheme of his own for doing away with all ancient rights and privileges in the town and the country alike, and for reducing the whole territory beneath his absolute sway. Under pretence of repressing heresy, and protecting the see against disaffection, it was his aim, namely, to collect a body of mercenaries from outside, to fall upon his own subjects, and by a display of severity to reduce them to an abject submission. "The burghers," he is reported to have said, "must be the first that I shall undo; then those of the country must follow."

In Tyrol, accordingly, whither he journeyed to do homage to his feudal superior, the Archduke Ferdinand, who was at Innsbruck, he engaged six companies of free-lances, alleging to the archduke as his excuse the necessity of being prepared against a possible Lutheran rising in his dominions. The citizens of Salzburg were horrified at the return of their liege lord with a small army at his back. Their alarm was increased on observing signs at the castle of the planting of ordnance in a position to threaten the town. So great was the panic that, on the peremptory demand of the cardinal-archbishop, the city surrendered at once unconditionally, and the prince-prelate rode in in triumph, followed by his retinue, to the guildhall on the bread market.

This entry lacked none of the pomp and magnificence characteristic of the age. The archbishop, clad in full armour, was mounted on a white charger, surrounded by his pages and courtiers, and followed by two companies of free-lances. A humble address delivered to the archbishop by the bürgermeister was answered by his chancellor in haughty and almost insulting language. All imperial charters, granting privileges to the town, were ordered to be surrendered, as well as those given by himself or by his predecessors. A formal document was then required to be drawn up and signed by the bürgermeister and principal councillors, pledging the town to submit in all things to the will of its feudal superior. Salzburg thus, unlike most of the other important towns of Germany, which had long ago settled accounts with their feudal overlords, was still in the throes of a struggle which, in not a few other cases, had been left two centuries behind. As a natural consequence, the class-antagonism within the walls, although unmistakably existing, was somewhat overshadowed. There was at least a solidarity of all classes against the feudal oppressor. A similar despotic policy was pursued throughout the whole territory of the archbishopric.

Severe persecutions of the preachers of the new gospel now followed. The recalcitrant priest, Matthaus, who had been amongst the most active of its propagandists, was sentenced to perpetual imprisonment. He was bound on a horse with an iron chain and was to be conveyed to a distant castle. On the way thither, however, his conductors turned into a friendly inn to refresh, leaving their prisoner alone outside. Finding a few peasants around him, attracted by curiosity, the preacher appealed to them to release him. In a short time a considerable crowd had gathered, and, a young peasant constituting himself leader, the preacher was released and went his way. The leader and another peasant engaged in this affair were afterwards secretly executed at Salzburg within the castle. , As soon as this was known, however, it acted as a powerful stimulus to the prevailing disaffection. The friends of the victims and of the new doctrines went about from valley to valley, secretly urging the country-folk to defend the gospel and avenge innocent blood.

The measureless exactions of the Cardinal-Archbishop all helped in the same direction. Not only was the peasantry taxed up to the hilt, but heavy subsidies were demanded from the wealthy burghers of the town of Salzburg. Insults, oppressions, exactions, continued throughout the winter of 1524-1525. But, at the same time, here as elsewhere, the opposition, which was to break out in the spring in the form of open rebellion, was organising itself. This first took definite shape in the valley of Gastein. Fourteen "articles" were formulated by this peasant population, whom the celebrated "Twelve Articles" of Upper Swabia appear not yet to have reached. First and foremost, the free preaching of the gospel without human additions was demanded. The free election of preachers was also insisted upon. Furthermore, various imposts were to be done away with, notably the merchet (or due payable on the marriage of a son or daughter, the death due, the so-called small tithe, and many other things of a like nature. A righteous administration of justice — and especially that the judges should be independent of the lord and his bailiffs — was also amongst the demands. A further curious item was that the cost of the execution of criminals should not fall upon the rural community. Finally, the maintenance of public roads for the facility of trade and intercourse was required.

On the basis of these articles, a "Christian Brotherhood" was formed here also. Messengers were sent into all the neighbouring valleys to secure adhesion. Soon the whole of the Alpine archbishopric was in motion, and by the end of April the insurrection had reached Styria, Carinthia and Upper Austria. The "Christian Brotherhood" was now well-established in all the Austrian lands.

The Archduke Ferdinand, who held court at Innsbruck, at this time called together the assembly of the Estates of the five Austrian Duchies to consider what action should be taken. The local assemblies of the territories also met. It was generally admitted on all sides that the revolt was brought about by high-handed and oppressive action on the part of the territorial magnates. Here, indeed, even the lower nobility, when offering the archduke their aid in quelling the insurrection, made the redress of certain specified wrongs, under which the "common man" was suffering, a necessary condition. The archduke himself had to agree. His real views and inclinations as regards the situation were probably better expressed by himself and the court-council at Vienna to the effect that "the crime must be chastised with a rod of iron, to the end that the evil and wanton device of the peasants should be punished, so that others may take warning thereby, also that those who are elsewhere already rebellious may be stilled and brought into submission. It is therefore our counsel and good opinion that ye all do proceed against all chiefs and leaders, wheresoever they may arise, or show themselves, with spearing, flaying, quartering, and every cruel punishment."

In Styria, Sigmund von Dietrichstein, who ten years before had mercilessly suppressed a peasant insurrection in the duchy (cf. German Society, pp.82-86) held still the chief authority in the land. He was, however, without men. Even the mercenaries sent him from Vienna refused to march against the peasantry, a section of them actually deserting to the latter. He would have been absolutely powerless, had not a contingent of three hundred Bohemian men-at-arms arrived upon the scene. An attempt, nevertheless, to attack a peasant encampment at Goysen resulted in the repulse and flight of his whole force. In his retreat through a narrow defile, the sides of which were occupied by parties of insurgents, Dietrichstein suffered almost more than in the open field. He himself was wounded, and confessed to a loss of over a hundred men killed, though this was undoubtedly far below the true number. To make matters worse, his remaining men now mutinied, and it was only with difficulty, and with the expenditure of a large sum of money, that he could induce them to remain with him. Two companies of free-lances and some three hundred horsemen were, however, on their way from Carinthia to his assistance. With the aid of these he was able to maintain his position, though he did not dare to attack the main body of rebels, consisting of some six thousand peasants. under the leadership of one Reustl. His attempts at negotiations, though they first of all failed owing to the opposition of Reustl, were eventually successful, the majority of the contingent deserting their leader and accepting the terms offered. Reustl, with a band of faithful followers, mostly workers in the salt mines, made good his retreat, and succeeded in reaching the main Salzburg contingent, which he joined.

By this time, things were getting hotter than ever in the archbishopric. The main body of the insurgent peasants were encamped in a village a few miles from Salzburg. They were armed with the most motley weapons, clubs, pitchforks and sickles, with only here and there a rusty sword or spear or a worn-out piece of armour. In this way they streamed forth from their valleys and mountain pastures. The episcopal functionaries were taken by surprise. They had omitted to occupy the leading pass. In vain the archbishop altered his tone; in vain he became mild, persuasive and even fatherly. The peasants were not so boorish as not to know the worth of his assurances. The townspeople of Salzburg were in full sympathy with them. So threatening did matters become that Matthaus Lang felt himself no longer safe in his palace on the market-place, and made good his retreat to his castle immediately above. A steep and narrow path led from the city to this impregnable fortress, which boasted a double wall, in part hewn out of the natural rock. The south side rested on a sheer precipice of 440 feet. Here the archbishop was safe enough as regards his person, but the position was not favourable for conducting negotiations with the town, in which his whole force consisted of one of the companies afore-mentioned, under the command of two knights named Schenk and Thurn. As in the case of the Frauenberg, members of his council were active in riding to and fro between the castle and the town, with the object of establishing a pact with the citizens.

The peasants kept in close touch with the Salzburgers. The chief intermediary of the latter with their overlord was a municipal functionary of the name of Gold. He was, however, suspected of treachery. One day, as the archbishop's military commanders, Hans Schenk and Sigmund von Thurn, were endeavouring to appease a tumultuous general assembly of the citizens on the market-place, Hans Gold was seen on horseback in the neighbourhood. Believing him to be acting the spy, or swayed by motives of personal vengeance, a butcher, against whom Gold had given an unfair decision in his judicial capacity, dragged him off his horse by the hook of his halberd. He was only prevented from running him through by the intervention of a brewer named Pickler. The incident was, nevertheless, a signal for the assembly to become openly insurrectionary; so much so that Schenk and Thurn themselves, fearing that their force was insufficient for the emergency, made a dash for the castle. Gold himself was not so fortunate, being seized and thrown into one of the towers, where he was put to the torture and had to confess matters concerning the archbishop's policy not calculated to conciliate the popular feeling. Finding that their official leaders had abandoned them, the company of free-lances were nothing loth to allow themselves to be enrolled in the service of the citizens.

The peasants now drew nearer the town, and on Whit Monday the brother of one of the peasants whom Lang had had secretly executed in his castle, entered the gates and rushed through the streets, affixing notices on the houses of the canons and councillors of the archbishop with the words: "This house is mine until the innocent blood of my brother be avenged". The same evening the main body of the peasants entered the city, the gates of which were thrown open to them. The usual scenes ensued on the following day; the palace of the prince-prelate on the market-place was entered; charters, documents and registers were destroyed, so that, as it was stated, one might wade knee-deep in the fragments; kitchens, cellars and dwelling-rooms were sacked, the retainers being turned out. By evening the building was empty, and became a place from the windows of which women hung their washing. In a few days, reinforcements arrived from the mining districts, well-armed and disciplined. Finding this to be the case, a large number of the original ill-armed contingent withdrew to their fields and villages, undertaking to maintain their newly-arrived comrades.

The insurgent city now set about laying siege in earnest to the archbishop and his nobles in the castle, the Hohen-Salzburg, as it was called. Every possible means of egress was occupied by them. They were, however, too late to prevent one of the prelatical councillors from riding off to solicit aid from the, courts of Bavaria and Austria. The Archduke was himself already too much pressed to afford any assistance, for in addition to his troubles previously spoken of in the so-called "five duchies," the movement had now reached Tyrol. As for the Duke of Bavaria, so far from being anxious to assist his brother potentate, he was disposed to treat secretly with the insurgents, with the view of obtaining possession of the Salzburg territories, and was only with difficulty prevented from carrying out this policy by the advice of his chancellor, Leonhard von Eck.

The Tyrolese movement is remarkable as being the only one of which it can be said that it obtained ultimate success of a modified kind. With the rest, rapid and complete as seemed their success at first, as rapidly and completely were they crushed in a few weeks. The Tyrolese, on the other hand, not only succeeded in prolonging the struggle far into the summer of 1526, but, although the far-reaching aspirations of those engaged in the conflict were doomed to disappointment, the peasantry as a whole did not go out altogether empty-handed. They obtained certain distinct concessions of a permanent nature. This was partly due, no doubt, to the intrepid character of the inhabitants, accustomed as they were from the earliest ages to a life of comparative freedom and independence; partly also to the formation of the country, in many parts inaccessible to any but natives, and everywhere easily capable of defence by small bands, and, last but not least, to the remarkable man who was not only the intellectual head of the movement, but who was as eminent as an organiser and diplomatist as he was bold and logical as a thinker — I refer to Michael Gaismayr.

On the Tyrolese insurrection, it may be worth while to quote here a report of a hostile contemporary witness, George Kirchmair (apud Jansen, vol. ii., pp.492-494 "There arose," writes Kirchmair, "a cruel, fearful, inhuman insurrection of the common peasant-folk in this land, at which I was at hand and beheld many wonders. Certain noisy, base people did adventure with violence to free from the judge a condemned rebel who had done mischief and who justly had been ordained to the penalty. After that they had done this thing on a Wednesday, did the peasants run together out of all mountains and valleys on Whit Sunday, young and old, albeit they knew not what they would do. As then a great concourse was come together in the Muklander Au within the Eisack valley, their conclusion was to free themselves from their oppression. A noble gentleman, Sigmund Brandisser, bailiff at Rodenegg, went straightway to the assembled peasants and showed to them all the danger, vanity, mischief, trouble and care. Notwithstanding that they promised him not to go forward to deeds, but to bring their complaint before their rightful prince, who was then in Innsbruck, yet did they not keep their promise, but on Whit Sunday at night made assault to Brixen, plundering and robbing in defiance of God and right, all priests, canons and chaplains. Thereafter did they assemble before the bishop's court and drave thence his councillors and his servants, with much violence, and in such inhuman manner that one may not write thereof. They of Brixen had as soon forgotten their duty toward Bishop Sebastian as the peasants of the new foundation toward their lord, the Prior Augustin. In fine, was there no duty, faith, vow, or other thing whatsoever bethought. The Brixeners and the peasants were of one mind. Every part had its chief men. These chiefs did without any cause or any renunciation (of allegiance) move with five thousand men against the monastery of the new foundation, and overran the priory on Friday, the 12th of May, 1525. Of the wantonness which they there wrought, a man might write a whole book. Prior Augustin, a pious man, was driven out and pursued, and the priests in such wise despised, mocked and tormented, that they must forsooth be made ashamed of the priestly sign and name. More than twenty-five thousand florins of loss in houses, silver, treasure, furnishings and eating vessels, charters and books, did the peasants bring about. No man may say with how much pride, drunkenness, blaspheming and sacrilege the priory was at this time offended. It had also been burned, had not God willed it otherwise. On Saturday, the 13th of May, they chose a captain, a fair-spoken yet cunning man, named Michael Gaismayr, son of a squire of Sterzing, an evil, a rebellious, but a cunning man. So soon as he was chosen their captain, the plundering of priest went on in the whole land. There was no priest so poor in the land but that he must lose all that was his own. Thereafter fell they upon divers nobles and did destroy so many that no man could or would arm himself to resist them; nay, even the Archduke Ferdinand and his most excellent wife held themselves nowhere saved. For in this whole land, in the valley of the Inn and of the Etsch, there was in the towns and amongst the peasants such a concourse, cry, and tumult, that hardly might a good man walk in the streets. Robbing, plundering and stealing did become so common that even not a few pious men were tempted thereto, who afterwards bitterly repented. And I speak the truth when I say that through this robbing, plundering and stealing, did no man wax rich."

A spy of the Archbishop of Trier reports to his master that emissaries from the Tyrolese insurgents were to be found in southern Germany and in Elsass, seeking to establish communications and an understanding between the two movements. He cautions his master at the same time, probably with the fear of Michael Gaismayr's constitutional reforms before his eyes, not to be deceived by the comparatively harmless "articles" of the peasants, for that something quite different lay behind these.

The Tyrolese peasantry had been stirring already, a few years before the great outbreak. They complained of much having been promised, but little carried out, by their lords and rulers. One of their great grievances was the prohibition of the killing of game. This prohibition, at last, they openly disregarded, and so impossible did it become to rehabilitate it that the Austrian Government at Innsbruck formally conceded the right of every peasant to hunt and shoot game on his own land. But, here as elsewhere, the embitterment of the people against nobles and clergy had gone too far to be appeased by partial concessions. In the mining districts, especially those belonging to the Fugger family at Schwatz, where the capitalistic wage-system was apparently first introduced, wages are said to have been in arrear at this time to the extent of forty thousand gulden. Add to this that the imperial council had recently put on an additional tax.

The new religious doctrines had soon obtained adherents in the Tyrol, especially amongst the miners. Foremost of the preachers were Johannes Strauss and Urbanus Regius. The evil life of princes and great ones was, of course, denounced. The rights proclaimed by the new jurists were likewise attacked as heathenish, and as not binding on Christian men. The year of jubilee was declared to be an institution still in force. Many other doctrines of a like nature were promulgated. A friar left his cell and engaged himself as a workman in the Fugger mines, in order to follow out the scriptural injunction to earn bread by the sweat of his brow. Here he had a taste of the newly-introduced wages-system for profit.

Followers of Thomas Münzer, or at least persons holding similar views, appeared also about this time in the valleys in question. Finally, these mining and peasant communities assembled together in the usual manner and drew up nineteen "articles" of reform. Most of these "articles" deal with the right of preaching the Gospel and other rights identical with those demanded elsewhere. The novel points were protests against the constant passage of armed men through the country and the quartering of alien troops in the frontier villages. One of the complaints was directed against the free exportation of the wines of Trient; another against the reckless riding of lords over cultivated fields; another against the new lawyer class; yet another against the keeping of wine-rooms by the judges and clerks of tribunals. Most noteworthy of all was a remonstrance against the Fugger family and against other privileged companies of merchants, which through their agents produced such a great increase in the cost of provisions that many articles had risen in price from eighteen kreutzers to a gulden. The assembled country people gave also, as one of the immediate causes of their action in coming together, the attempted removal by the authorities of certain ordnance and ammunition, which removal, however, it would appear, they had been successful in preventing. Zimmermann conjectures that they feared that the war-material in question was to be used against their brethren who had risen in the neighbouring provinces.

The concessions of the archduke had their effect for the moment. Most of the rural communities consented to await the Landtag which was to consider their grievances. This applies to the Tyrol itself, but not to the Vorarlberg. In and around Bregenz the insurrection gathered, until it soon numbered forty thousand men, who insultingly replied to the emissaries from the archducal court at Innsbruck that they would come in a few days and bring the answer themselves to the proposals made.

In the south also, the movement showed no signs of abating. As we have seen, the source and centre of the Tyrolese rising was the neighbourhood of the town of Brixen, many public functionaries there joining the cause. Michael Gaismayr himself had been the bishop's secretary and the keeper of the customs at Klausen. From the proceeds of the sacking of the wealthy house of the Teutonic Order at Bozen, Gaismayr, now elected captain of the local contingent, formed the nucleus of a war-chest. It was augmented by numerous other spoliations of ecclesiastical possessions. Gaismayr, further, at once opened up a correspondence with the view of gathering into his hand the threads of agitation in the surrounding territories. In his manifestoes he knew how to combine in the cleverest way the immediate aspirations and the popular demands of those with whom he was dealing, whilst hinting at the more far-reaching projects of the Christian commonwealth that formed his ultimate goal. For example, he knew how to exploit patriotic sentiment by pointing out the evils resulting from the occupation of important posts by aliens, notably by Spaniards, whose promotion Charles V. and his brother had naturally favoured.

Under Gaismayr the insurrection rapidly spread, in spite of the archduke's blandishments and the temporary character of the peasants' success in certain interior districts of the Tyrol itself. From the lake of Garda and Trient in the south, the whole country soon broke out into open and organised revolt. One peasant camp was formed outside the city of Trient itself. Other contingents swept the valleys of the Brixen territories and of the Etsch, plundering monasteries and castles, and occupying the smaller towns or laying them under contribution. Gaismayr's headquarters were at Meran. With him were the delegates of the towns and of the various jurisdictions of the Tyrol province, endeavouring with difficulty to reconcile local demands with one another and with the general object of the movement. Loyalty to the feudal chiefs of the province, the house of Austria, seems to have been deeply ingrained in the hearts of the countryfolk, and, in spite of his own ultimate end, Gaismayr was careful not to openly collide with, or even disregard, this feeling. Although the local nobility and clergy were everywhere regarded as fair game for plunder and rapine, the agrarians were particularly concerned to spare the archduke's castles.

Meanwhile, the archduke himself continued to adopt a conciliatory and even friendly tone in his messages. It is said that he had really an affection for his patrimonial province, but in any case he had no force of fighting men at hand with which to quell the revolted populations. That this latter motive was chiefly responsible for his mildness is evidenced by the fact that he gave orders to the Innsbruck council to negotiate a loan by the pledging of certain lands and jewellery for the purpose of raising the force he wanted. At the same time he sought to hurry on the promised Landtag.

Gaismayr, on his side, had called a Landtag, which, however, was forbidden by the archduke by special messengers with signed and sealed despatches. On the despatches being read, the majority of the peasant council at Meran accepted the armistice and abandoned the projected Landtag, which was to have been held at that place. But difficulties arose when it was found that the Austrian Government did not interpret the armistice as implying any duty on its part to abstain from further armaments. In a special rescript to the imperial authorities, written about this date by the archduke, the latter lets his mask of mildness fall, complaining that the machinations of the evil-minded populations were such that they would allow no foreign mercenaries to enter the country, that he himself was practically a prisoner in his own land, and that from day to day there was no certainty that the capital, Innsbruck itself, would not be attacked.

The insurrection was master throughout the duchy. On the calling of the Landtag at Innsbruck, a hundred and six "articles," formulated by the standing council at Meran, probably under Gaismayr's direction, were submitted, and the archduke was compelled to concede a number of points that must have proved very sour to him. These were finally brought together in the form of a new constitution for the province, containing strong and democratic provisions. But further demands were made in many quarters, and the insurrection, everywhere smouldering, burst out into renewed activity in several districts.

We must now, for the present, leave the fortunes of the Tyrolese, in order to turn to those of the movement in west Austrian lands and in the Alsatian and Rhenish districts abutting on them. It is impossible to separate, either topographically or historically, the hither Austrian dominion of Breisgau from the Margravate of Baden and the adjoining districts. The Black Forest contingent, under Hans Müller von Bulgenbach, moved westward early in May for the purpose of combining with contingents which had formed, in the latter part of April, in the Austrian territory and in the Margravate, and of making a combined attack upon the important city of Freiburg, one of the best defended and most noteworthy towns of south-west Germany. Breisgau and Baden had been in a state of fermentation for a year past. Local disturbances and a threatened general rising are recorded from the early summer of 1524 onwards. By the end of that year, large numbers of nobles and clerics, apprehending anew "Bundschuh," had fled into Freiburg for security, amongst them the Markgraf Ernst, with his wife and children. Freiburg had, therefore, become a nest of the privileged classes and a repository of vast treasures.

The chief of the Margravate contingent was one Hans Hammerstein. In dread of an attack by Hammerstein upon his castle of Rotelen, the Markgraf had taken to flight. Rotelen, however, did not share the fate of so many other strongholds of Baden, and was reserved for destruction in the second half of the seventeenth century during the wars of Louis XIV. Arrived at Freiburg, the Markgraf sent conciliatory letters, accompanied by offers of mediation on the part of the Freiburg authorities. But, unlike his brother Philip, a man of exceptional humanity for that age, and immensely popular with his subjects, Ernst was mistrusted, and could not succeed in making any impression with his overtures. After discussing the matter in conclave, the peasants returned answer that if he would unreservedly countersign the "Twelve Articles," and regard himself henceforward as no more than the trustee and vicegerent of the emperor, he might retain his castle and his lands. If, on the other hand, he refused to consider himself as primus inter pares of themselves, it would go badly with him, since they were determined to have done with nobles, to have nobody in authority over them save peasants like themselves, and to acknowledge no lord but the emperor. These proposals obviously did not suit this wealthy territorial magnate, who, finding himself in security for the time being, was content to let matters drift.

The practical refusal of the Markgraf to concede anything resulted in a rising of the whole land. All the important castles, including Rotelen, were occupied. A camp of peasant contingents was formed at Heidersheim. The wealthy monastery of Thennenbach was stripped, suffering damage, as was alleged, to the amount of thirty thousand golden, whilst the small town of Kenzingen was taken and garrisoned, and the arrival was awaited of Hans Müller with his contingent before Freiburg.

Freiburg was at its wits' end, and was well-nigh denuded of fighting men, having a few weeks previously sent some bodies of free-lances in its service to the assistance of other towns more immediately threatened than itself. The Schlossberg, the great stronghold commanding the town, was manned by no more than a hundred and twenty-four men. All available persons, however, who were in the town, made ready to assist in its defence, and all flaws in the fortifications were repaired. The authorities then sent out to know the meaning of the presence of Hans Müller and the Black Forest contingent in the Breisgau territory. The reply was an expression of regret that Freiburg should be on the side of the oppressors of the "common man," and of hope that the city would enter the "Evangelical Brotherhood". To this the city answered that its oath to the House of Austria prevented its undertaking such obligations as those suggested, but professed its willingness to mediate where special grievances could be shown, and concluded with hoping that the Black Forest peasants, mindful of how divine and blessed it was to live in peace, would withdraw themselves from the neighbourhood of Breisgau. Hans Müller, thereupon, declared that his Black Forest men were not acting without the concurrence of their brethren, the Breisgau peasants. He then moved his camp into the city's immediate proximity.

By the 17th of May, the local contingents also arrived before Freiburg, from the battlements of which the banners of twenty companies were to be counted. Accordingly, the forces being now joined, an ultimatum was sent on this day requiring the formal alliance of Freiburg with the

"Evangelical Brotherhood". No answer was returned, and the siege began by the close investment of the city. Aqueducts were constructed to draw off the water. The block-house on the Schlossberg was taken by surprise a day or two later, and, as some nobles were sitting on a fine May evening drinking their wine before a hostelry in the cathedral close, five hundred shots fell around them. The fighting power of the town was forthwith drawn up in readiness on the fish-market. The citizens were divided into twelve companies corresponding to the twelve guilds, each of which had to defend its own gate, tower and section of the wall. Even the University supplied its company, consisting of some forty students under the leadership of the rector and two professors. Help from without was nowhere forthcoming. The civic authorities thus expressed themselves in a report made later on, "No man did come to our help. From Hegau to Strasburg, and thence from Würtemberg to the Welsh (French) country we had no friends. All townships, hamlets and villages were against us."

On the evening of the 21st, a further ultimatum from the peasants was sent into the town. They only wished well to the country, but demanded "a goodly Christian order and the freeing of the common man from excessive and unjust burdens ". Meanwhile, within the town, ominous voices made themselves heard in the guildrooms. Freiburg was not in a position to sustain a long siege, and the idea of its being taken by assault was not palatable to the wealthy citizens. Moreover, sympathy with the peasant cause, though not so widely spread as in some other towns, was not wanting, and there were many poor citizens who had friendly relations with the besiegers without the walls. The upshot was that on the 24th of May, a week after the siege had been begun, Freiburg capitulated and agreed to enter the "Evangelical Brotherhood".

Both sides pledged themselves to do their utmost to further a general peace, and the removal of the burdens of the "common man," and also to cherish the true principles of the Gospel. The relations of the town to its feudal overlord were not to be compromised, nor its liberty in any way curtailed. It was to pay to the assembled contingents the sum of three thousand golden as earnest of its good intentions. This sum was afterwards increased, and further pecuniary demands were made. Freiburg appears also to have supplied the peasants with some artillery, for in an exculpatory report, subsequently made to the Austrian Government, we read: "We have indeed loaned the peasants four falconets, the which had no great worth, but yet for no other end than that they might hold the Rhine at Limburg against the Welsh (the foreigners). For we have given the commandment to the twain to whom we delivered them that they should destroy this ordnance so soon as there were danger against any other person soever." Thus ended the peasant siege of Freiburg.

The attention of the peasant bodies was at this time drawn off from Freiburg and Breisgau generally to the disasters that were befalling their cause in the neighbouring Elsass. Even the strongly-fortified town of Breisach they were content to leave, after having threatened it for some days, on a pledge being given that no foreign troops should be permitted to cross the river at any point within the defensive capacity of the town.

The attack on the town of Villingen was repulsed, the garrison making sorties and razing the peasant homesteads near by Rudolfzell, which, as we have seen, had received into its walls numbers of fugitive nobles, who constituted its main armed force, had also compelled the Black Foresters to retire. A body of knights, in fact, in making a sortie, distinguished themselves by burning the neighbouring villages and throwing women and children into the flames. An agreement was ultimately made through the mediation of the popular and amiable Markgraf Philip of Baden, who also acted on behalf of his brother Ernst. It consisted of the following two articles: (1) that the great tithe should be rendered as of wont, but, until the judgment of the mutter, should be laid by in a neutral place, while the small tithe should not be rendered until this judgment, and that corvées should also cease meanwhile; (2) that all the ordnance of the Markgraf and all other that might be in the hands of the peasant bodies should be brought into the town of Neuenburg, should be there preserved until the issue of the matter, and should be by neither side used against the other.

About this time — the middle of June — further understandings as regards an armistice were entered into between the various contingents and Freiburg, Breisach, Offenburg, and other towns of Breisgau and Baden.

We now turn to the contiguous, and in many respects allied, movement in Elsass. Here the insurrection began, as elsewhere, early in April. It spread like wild-fire from town to town and from village to village. A contemporary, writing from Strasburg at the end of April, says: "The peasants have everywhere assembled themselves in companies. They hold the most towns and divers castles. The Papists are in a fear such as is not to be believed. The rich are filled with alarm for their treasure, and even we in our strong town live not wholly without dread."

Iconoclasm was the order of the day in Strasburg. Churches were ransacked; monks and nuns were driven out of cloister and convent. The city, in fact, was at one time in imminent danger of falling into the hands of the rebels. The council, however, appears to have got wind of a conspiracy to introduce the armed peasants into the town, and sixteen worthy burghers were in consequence arrested, some of them paying for their temerity with their lives. Unfortunately, throughout Elsass many priceless works of mediaeval art were destroyed in the pillaging; pictures, wood carvings, and the contents of monastic libraries being often used for the lighting of fires.

On the 28th of April the "United Contingent of Elsass," as it was called, which numbered 20,000 men, commanded by one Erasmus Gerber, marched along a mountain ridge, constituted by a spur of the Vosges, to attach the town of Zabern, the residence of the Bishop of Strasburg. Zabern, although comparatively small, was well fortified, and was calculated to form a most valuable base and storehouse for the insurgent forces. Their first objective was the wealthy abbey of Mauersmünster, between two and three miles from Zabern. The foundation was completely sacked from cellar to roof. An establishment of the Teutonic Order was also sacked, and a valuable booty was obtained. In fact, the insurgent camp glittered with chalices, salvers, church utensils, and decorations of all sorts. Zabern was then challenged to open its gates and join the Peasant League. The canons and the patrician councillors wished to send for help to Duke Antoine of Lorraine, who on the first symptoms of danger had offered to throw a garrison into the town. The bulk of the citizens, however, declared that they would rather open their gates to the peasants than to these Frenchmen. They refused to receive any aliens at all. Finally, after some negotiations, the gates were opened, and the peasant army entered Zabern on the 13th of May, occupying the fortifications with a strong force, and also entrenching themselves immediately outside the walls.

Far-reaching plans seem to have been talked of at this time of the invasion of France and of the humiliation of the French seigneur like the German adelige. The impression seems to have prevailed that the whole strength of the French noblesse had been exhausted at the battle of Pavia. The importance of the capture of Zabern was hardly to be exaggerated, and Duke Antoine hurried on his preparations for crushing the rebels. Weissenburg was from the very first entirely in their hands, even the bürgermeister and the majority of the council being on the insurgent side, together with the powerful vintners' guild, to which most of the councillors belonged.

The formula of the peasants was to demand, "in the name of Jesus Christ Our Lord," that every town, hamlet and village should furnish their fourth man to the contingent. As we have seen in a former chapter, the demands put forward in Elsass were considerably more drastic than the celebrated "Twelve Articles". An agent of the Archbishop of Trier reports to his master that the "common man" of the towns was far more violent even than the peasant. "With one accord," he writes, "cry they: "we will not alone win monasteries and castles; but will have our hands busy in the towns, and there also will we be as gentlemen'." He alleges that they had definite relations with the Breisgau and Black Forest contingents.

The movement did not leave the town of Colmar untouched. The discontented here formulated fourteen "articles," which they laid before the council. The matter was quieted for a time, but in the second week of April renewed disturbances took place. The insurrection, however, did not succeed in making any headway within the walls, and in spite of repeated threats the gates remained closed to the peasants. Colmar in fact at this time, like many other towns that had successfully resisted invasion, was full of fugitives glad to save the wreck of their property. Jews were especially in evidence.

From Elsass, the movement spread along the Rhine. On the 23rd of April, in a village in the neighbourhood of Landau, on the occasion of a kirchaweith (church-ale), a peasant band formed itself, which subsequently developed into the so-called Geilweiler contingent. Emissaries from the band went round all the neighbouring villages, visited the peasants in their houses, and even fetched them out of their beds, persuading or compelling them to join the ranks. The band almost immediately began the pillaging of monasteries and other ecclesiastical foundations. They took therefrom "corn, wine, cattle and victuals, and lived in wantonness," says a contemporary chronicler. The neighbouring castles shared the same fate. Such an enormous amount of spoil was collected, that the half of it had to be left behind in a village through which the contingent passed. Day by day their numbers swelled. Feeling themselves strong enough now to proceed to greater things, they summoned, on Sunday, the 13th of April, the little, well-fortified town of Neustadt to surrender. The Rhenish Elector in vain admonished the citizens to hold no converse with "the wanton, lawless band". The Bishop of Speyer, who counted a large number of his own villeins in the contingent, also interposed without effect.

At the beginning of 'May another body formed near Lauterburg, the captain being the bürgermeister of that place. The bishop was forced to concede to them the entry into one or two strongholds, on their professing to have no disloyal sentiments towards himself, but only to wish to defend the territory against the foreigner. In Lauterburg, high festival was held. The overhanging castle was broken into, and, according to a contemporary account, "the women from the villages hard by did come into the castles and did drink themselves so full of wine that they might no more walk". Meanwhile the town of Landau itself had become the prey of the Geilweiler contingent, and had to hand over all the corn and wine in its possession, most of which had been entrusted to its care by various neighbouring monasteries. Two peasant delegates from each company were sent into the town to see that there was no cheating in this transaction.

A band now formed in the neighbourhood of Worms which swept the country round, receiving the adhesion of all the villages through which it passed. On learning of the approach of the Marshal of the Palatinate, Wilhelm von Habern, with a force of three hundred horse and five hundred foot, they established themselves in a strong position in a vine-clad hill above the little town of Westhofen. The marshal was prevented by the favourable position of the peasants from making a direct attack, but he had no sooner fired three shots into their camp than they fled into the village below — a flight that cost the lives of sixty of them, at the hands of the marshal's men. During the night they retreated to Neustadt, where they united with the Geilweiler contingent.

The Elector Ludwig, besides being unable for want of men to suppress the rising by force, showed signs of his being sincerely desirous of an amicable arrangement with his subjects. Through the mediation of the town of Neustadt, an interview was arranged between the elector and the peasant leaders in a field outside the village of Forst. It was stipulated, however, that the elector should be accompanied by no more than thirty horsemen as his retinue. As soon as the parties were met, the whole of the peasant forces appeared on the brow of an elevation a little way off.

This was evidently a device of the leaders to overawe the elector. After protracted negotiations, it was agreed that the towns, castles and villages taken should be surrendered to their lawful lords and masters, that no further hostile acts should be committed, and that the peasant bands, which here numbered some 8,000 men, should disperse to their homes. On his side, the Elector Ludwig promised the peasants a complete amnesty, and, in addition, the calling at an early date of a Landtag, at which their grievances should be considered and remedied.

Thereupon the elector retired for the night to Neustadt. The following day, on representatives of the peasants announcing themselves with a view of obtaining a definite promise as to the date of the Landtag in question, the elector not only satisfied their demands, but invited them to his table. "There," in the words of Harer, a contemporary historian of the war, "one saw villeins and their lord sit together, and eat and drink together. He had, so it seemed, one heart to them and they to him."

The Landtag was then convened for the week after Whitsuntide. Its decisions were to be binding throughout the whole country, that is to say, on both sides of the Rhine. The seemingly mild, and even generous conduct of the elector did not, however, entirely quell the insurrection. General excitement and the temptation of plunder were too great. Bands of peasants throughout the Palatinate continued the old course of pillage and destruction. It was not until the common suppression of the movement that these bands dispersed, and the Palatinate settled down to its wonted state. Similarly, in the adjacent bishopric of Speyer, in spite of agreements, it was not until the advance of Truchsess and the forces of the Swabian League that all hostilities on the side of the peasants came to an end.

Chapter VII. The Thuringian Revolt and Thomas Münzer.

We come now to speak of the figure most prominently associated by tradition and the popular mind with the Peasants War. In the view of most persons, the whole movement that we are describing centres in the figure of the schoolmaster and preacher who came from Stolberg in the Hartz Mountains. For weal or for woe, history seems to have indelibly stamped the last great peasant revolt of the Middle Ages with the name of Thomas Münzer. Yet it may be fairly doubted whether the stupendous influence on the events of the year 1525 attributed by historical tradition to the personality in question has not been very much exaggerated.

That Münzer, in the winter of 1524-5, made a tour of agitation through central and southern Germany, including those districts where the revolt earliest broke out, is undoubtedly true, but we find, if we analyse the accounts, that the reception of his preaching was by no means everywhere encouraging. Thus Melancthon, in his pamphlet Historia Thoma Müntzers, etc., expressly states that the Franconians, who, as we have seen, played such a zealous and important part in the movement, would have none of Münzer or his doctrine. It is, of course, perfectly true that the object of the malignant toady Melancthon in writing this political manifesto, was to curry favour with the victorious princes and to defame Münzer's character. But, seeing that the whole trend of the work in question is to display Münzer in the role of a powerful and dangerous demagogue, as, in fact, a kind of arch-fiend of rebellion, Melancthon can have had no conceivable object in making the above statement. Moreover, a statement of this kind, not referring to an obscure episode in a man's life, but to his public activity of a few months before, if untrue, must have been so notoriously untrue as not to have been worth the stating. Hence, in the absence of rebutting evidence which does not seem forthcoming, we can hardly do otherwise than accept it. Other accounts, which speak of Münzer's influence in south Germany, especially in the Klettgau and the Hegau, leave it uncertain how far they refer to Münzer himself and how far to those preaching similar doctrines — doctrines unquestionably in the air at the time, and not exclusively ascribable to any single man.

Turning from Münzer as agitator to Münzer as thinker, the same tendency to exaggeration with otherwise accurate and sober-minded historians is often to be found. Münzer is represented as an embodiment not only of the practical movement of the time but also of its idealistic side. That he energetically championed the chiliastic notion of a Christian Commonwealth, then so generally prevalent amongst the thinking heads of the revolt, is true enough. But, on the other hand, we fail to discover in his extant writings anything more than vague aspirations towards it; there is certainly nothing approaching the originality of handling, and the elaboration of the idea, exhibited by Michael Gaismayr. We find this even in the pamphlet where the social views of Münzer are most prominent, his "Emphatic Exposure of the False Belief of the Faithless World" ("Aussgetruckte emplossung des falschen Glaubens der ungetrewen Welt"), published at Mühlhausen late in 1524. Here also all we have is a vague expression of belief in the necessity of the establishment of a communistic society and in its approaching advent.

Münzer strikes us as before everything a theologian. This is noticeable in his pamphlets down to the very eve of the Peasants War. In the one on the ordering of the German mass at Allstatt, in another on the book of Daniel, and in an exposition of the nineteenth Psalm — the last published in 1525 — we see him most concerned to justify his ecclesiastical innovations and his theories respecting infant baptism, the Eucharist, and other edifying theological topics. He speaks, indeed, at times bitterly enough of the oppression of prince, noble and prelate, and of the right of the "common man" to rebel, but, we repeat, there is no evidence of any constructive theory beyond the most casual expressions. Of course, in saying this, we by no means forget that his main strength lay in his fervid oratory, and that his influence from this point of view was considerable. All we contend is that, as in so many historical cases, chance has played kindly with his fame, and has obtained for him credit for an influence, theoretical and practical, over the general movement of 1525 which the cold light of research hardly seems to justify.

Thomas Münzer appears to have been born in the last decade of the fifteenth century. An uncertain tradition states that his father was hanged by the Count of Stolberg. The first we hear of him with certainty is as teacher in the Latin school at Aschersleben and afterwards at Halle. Where he studied is doubtful, but by this time he had already graduated as doctor. In Halle he is alleged to have started an abortive conspiracy against the Archbishop of Magdeburg. In 1515 we find him as confessor in a nunnery and afterwards as teacher in a foundation school at Brunswick. Finally, in 1520, he became preacher at the Marienkirche at Zwickau, and here his public activity in the wider sense really began. The democratic tendencies previously displayed by him broke all bounds. He thundered against those who devoured widows' houses and made long prayers and who at death-beds were concerned not with the faith of the dying but with the gratification of their measureless greed.

At this time Münzer was still a follower of Luther, but it was not long before he found him a lukewarm church-reformer. Luther's bibliolatry, as opposed to his own belief in the continuous inspiration of certain chosen men by the Divine spirit, excited his opposition. He criticised still more severely as an unpardonable inconsistency Luther's retention of certain dogmas of the old Church whilst rejecting others. He now began to study with enthusiasm the works of the old German mystics, Meister Eck and Johannes Tauler, and more than all those of Joachim Floras, the Italian enthusiast of the twelfth century. A general conviction soon came uppermost in his mind of the necessity of a thorough revolution alike of Church and State.

His mystical tendencies were strengthened by contact with a sect which had recently sprung up amongst the clothworkers of Zwickau, and of which one Nicholas Storch, a master clothworker, was corypheus. The sect in question lived in a constant belief in the approach of a millennium to be brought about by the efforts of the "elect". Visions and ecstasies were the order of the day amongst these good people. This remarkable sect influenced various prominent persons at this time. Karlstadt was completely fascinated by them. Melancthon was carried away; and even Luther admits having had some doubts whether they had not a Divine mission. The worthy Elector Friedrich himself would take no measures against them, in spite of the dangerous nature of their teaching from the point of view of political stability. He was afraid, as he said "lest perchance he should be found fighting against God".

It was not long before Münzer allied himself with these "enthusiasts," or "prophets of Zwickau," as they were called. When the patrician council at Zwickau forbade the cloth-workers to preach, Münzer denounced the ordinance and encouraged them to disobey it. New prohibitions followed, culminating in prosecutions and imprisonments. The result was that, by the end of 1521, the cloth-working town had become too hot to hold the new reformers. Some fled to Wittenberg, and others, including Münzer himself, into Bohemia. Arrived in Prague, Münzer posted up an announcement in Latin and German that he would "like that excellent warrior of Christ, Johann Huns, fill the trumpets with a new song". He proceeded in his addresses to denounce the clergy, and to prophesy the approaching vengeance of heaven upon their order. He here also preached against the "dead letter," as he called it, of the Bible, expounding his favourite theory of the necessity of believing in the supplemental inspiration of all elect persons. But the soil of Bohemia proved not a grateful one. It had been exhausted by over a century of religious fanaticism and utopistic dreams of social regeneration.

The next we hear of Münzer is as preacher at Alstatt in Thuringia. Allstatt was the scene of his great Church reformation, in defence of which he published a pamphlet. The whole seance was conducted in the German language. All the books of the Bible were read and expounded in their order, instead of the isolated passages used in the Roman ritual. His success here was immense. Crowds streamed to hear him from the neighbouring towns and villages. He soon counted not a few theologians and other learned persons amongst his adherents. Great was the rush from all sides to listen to the popular preacher. As Münzer himself has it, "the poor thirsty folk did so yearn for the truth that all the streets were full of people come to hear it".

He was still, up to the spring of 1523, almost entirely a drastic Church reformer rather than a political or social revolutionist. He wrote repeatedly to the Elector Friedrich of Saxony and to his brother, Duke Johann, exhorting them as his "dearest, must beloved rulers," and warning them not to he deceived by hypocritical priests, but to boldly take their stand on the Gospel. Finding that his admonitions to those in authority produced no immediate effect, he turned with increasing zeal to the "common man". Although the religious side of Münzer's character probably remained the most prominent to the end, the political side now came distinctly to the fore. He founded a secret society at Allstatt pledged by a solemn oath to labour unceasingly for the promotion of the new kingdom of God on earth, a kingdom to be based on the model of the primitive Christian Church as he supposed it to have been. Freedom and equality must reign here. The princes and the great ones of the earth refused to espouse the cause of the new Gospel. Hence, they must be overthrown, and the "common man", who was prepared to embrace the Gospel, must be raised up in their place. He who would not become a citizen of the kingdom of God must be banished or killed. The great barrier to the awakening of the inward light was the riches of this world. Hence, in the kingdom of God, private wealth should cease to be, and all things should be in common.

Münzer now began to send out missionaries to different parts of Germany, and soon after established a special printing press in Allstatt for the publication of the pamphlets he was issuing. Whilst at this town he also, like Luther, married an escaped nun. As a result of his preaching against the worship of images, a chapel, a well-known place of pilgrimages near Allstatt, was burned to the ground. Called to account for this by Duke Johann, those responsible, Münzer at their head, refused to appear to answer for their action, justifying themselves by texts out of the Old Testament.

Finally, Elector Friedrich and Duke Johann came in person to the castle at Allstatt, where they summoned Münzer to preach before them and expound the doctrines that seemed so subversive of "social order". Münzer, obeying the summons, delivered an impassioned sermon, well stocked with Biblical quotations. In this discourse he vehemently demanded the death of all priests and monks who perverted the people and who stigmatised the Gospel preached by him as heresy. The godless, he said, had no right to live. If the princes refused themselves to exterminate the godless, God would take the sword from them and accomplish the work through others. He then proceeded to attack such social evils of the times as usury, oppression by princes and lords, and the appropriation by them of what of right belonged to the "common man," the fish in the water, the fowls of the air, the produce of the soil. While professing to protect the commandments of God, one of which said "Thou shah not steal," they themselves robbed without mercy the poor husbandmen and the poor craftsman. If the latter in their turn committed ought, be it never so little, against the property of their lords, they must forsooth hang for it. To all this iniquity, said he, your Doctor Liar — his favourite sobriquet for Luther — saith Amen.

The effect on his princely hearers may be imagined, an effect that was enhanced when Münzer immediately caused his discourse to be printed and circulated amongst their liege subjects. It does not appear that even now the mild and benevolent-minded prince-elector took any action, but Duke Johann at once ordered the printer to quit the territory. Münzer, in a document dated the 13th of July, 1524, protests against the attempt to prevent his freely expounding the doctrines with which the Divine Spirit had inspired him. He refused the invitation of Luther to debate with him at Wittenberg, alleging the undue influence of Luther's party in that town. He would not, he said, preach in a corner, but only before the people.

The new doctrines were now gall and wormwood to Luther, who had hurried hack from the Wartburg in the spring of 1523, on learning of the turn things were taking in Wittenberg owing to the doctrines of the Zwickau enthusiasts. In imminent fear of the Reformation getting beyond his control, he had succeeded by his strong personality and authority in stemming the tide, but only after he had made some outward concessions, at least, to the new tendencies. Thus, the German mass, the total abolition of images, and other innovations introduced by Karlstadt and his friends were reluctantly adopted by Luther. But the new political and social doctrines, represented by Münzer, Luther could not away with. In a letter to his patron, the prince-elector, against the rebellious spirit abroad, Luther entreats the princes to banish these unruly prophets. "Let them keep their hands still," said he, "or straightway be cast out of the land. Thus should he the speech of princes to the prophets. For Satan worketh through these misguided spirits." Münzer, not without reason, retorted on Luther that he (Luther) wished to hand over the Church he had torn from the Pope to the secular princes, and that he himself would fain be the new Pope. Luther's little dog, Melancthon, wrote to his friend Spalatin in tones of unctuous horror that the new preachers would make worldly politics of the Gospel. Territorial lords forbade their villeins to attend Münzer's preachmg.

A false disciple at this time betrayed Münzer's secret propagandist organisation to the authorities. The result was the citation of Münzer to the castle at Weimar once more to give an account of himself before the princes, this time on a direct accusation of incitement to rebellion. He went alone and ably defended himself when confronted with passages from his published tracts. The prince-elector still maintained his unwillingness to take active measures against the new doctrines, preferring, as he expressed it, to take his staff in hand and quit for ever his ancestral territories rather than risk doing aught against the will of God. Certainly, Prince Friedrich of Saxony is one of the very few potentates in history of whose complete sincerity and single-mindedness we can have no reasonable doubt. His brother, however, Duke Johann, and the councillors, threatened Münzer with peremptory expulsion from the land should he continue his present course. Münzer was then dismissed. As he descended from the castle he met one of his friends who was in the princely service. "How hath it gone with thee?" asked the latter. "It hath so gone with me," replied Münzer, "that I must needs seek another principality."

Münzer hurried hack to Allstatt, but only to find that the sworn enemy of the Reformation, the aggressively Catholic Duke George of Saxony, had interposed, demanding of the elector his deliverance into his hands, and threatening to interfere by force of arms if he were longer allowed to remain at Allstatt. At last the elector gave way to the extent of issuing an order to the town council of Allstatt to direct Münzer to leave that place. Münzer immediately quitted Allstatt for the neighbouring imperial city of Mühlhausen. This city, like the other Thuringian towns, notably Erfurt, had been profoundly excited by the events of the Reformation. Münzer here encountered the man who was destined to be his colleague in the noteworthy historical events that followed. This was Heinrich Pfeiffer, who was originally a monk in a neighbouring monastery, and had Luther-wise cast his cowl. He preached the new doctrines, first of all, in the territory of the Archbishop of Mainz. Driven thence he returned to his native town. Here he further carried on the work of a popular preacher and agitator.

One Sunday, as the public crier summoned the burghers to partake of beer and wine, he stood upon the stone when the crier quitted it, shouting: "Hear me, ye citizens; I will offer you another drink". He proceeded abusing the clergy, monks and nuns in the usual church reformer's manner. His discourse exciting attention, he promised to preach again from the same place next day. The city council in vain summoned him before them, he replying that he would first keep his word and deliver the promised speech. At its close, he deigned to appear at the Rathhaus, but accompanied by such a formidable crowd of sympathisers that the council (Rath) feared to take immediate steps against him.

Pfeiffer continued to preach at Mühlhausen, and his adherents increased every day. He now boldly demanded a guard of honour from the council, to ensure his safety from the enemies of the Gospel. This being naturally refused, he again ascended the stone of the public crier, and challenged the immense crowd assembled to indicate by holding up their hands their determination to stand by him and the Gospel. A forest of hands appeared in response. The matter now shaped itself as a conflict between the town population, zealous supporters of Pfeiffer, and the patrician council as zealous upholders of the old order in Church and State.

Pfeiffer soon became convinced of the need for a radical reformation of the council. What happened in other towns happened also in Mühlhausen. A non-official council or committee of the citizens was formed to oppose the Rath. Pfeiffer's chief claim was that the churches should cease to be the exclusive appanage of members of the "Teutonic Order", but should be occupied by competent preachers of the new doctrines. The Rath finally took the step of driving Pfeiffer from the town. A short time afterwards, however, he seems to have returned. The iconoclastic zeal of the citizens now took the form of the destruction of pictures and ornaments in the churches, but Pfeiffer appears to have taken little part in this action. His chief interest henceforth was the reform of the town government.

On the 24th of August, 1524, he was again driven from Mühlhausen. He now turned to the environs and the peasants. A document containing twelve "articles" was drawn up by him and presented to the Rath. The articles were probably the same as those which Münzer laid before his own contingent, claiming the confiscation of all the landed property of the Church, the abolition of corvées, the annulment of feudal dues that could not show a prescription of two hundred years, and the freedom of the chase and of fishing. Reform of the criminal law was also demanded, with what amounted to the abolition of the arbitrary jurisdiction of the territorial feudal lords. Finally, the election of the city council by the body of the citizens was claimed, with the power of revoking mandates. Eligibility should not be confined to members of the Geschlechter or old patrician families; at least a certain number of the council were to be ordinary guildsmen.

Münzer now arrived in Mühlhausen and constituted himself the leader of the town proletariat, just as Pfeiffer was already the successful champion of the guildsmen or main body of the citizens against the patrician Rath. The diversity of interests between the two classes and between the ultimate aims of the two men caused a certain amount of friction in the popular movement. Pfeiffer, as a representative of the small middle class, desired the destruction of feudalism for middle class purposes, but does not appear to have had any communistic sympathies. Münzer, on the contrary, as we have already seen, was now nothing if not a prophet of the Christian Commonwealth, or Kingdom of God on earth, of which communism, as understood in the Middle Ages, was an essential element. Hence the patrician party was able to force the assent of the requisite number of the body of the citizens to Münzer's expulsion. But that of Pfeiffer followed hard upon it, the Guildsmen having apparently become frightened at the intrusion of the extramural proletarians and the peasantry of the city territory into the movement. For it must not be forgotten that the two men, despite divergencies of ultimate purpose, worked hand in hand for the attainment of their immediate objects, Pfeiffer using the eloquence and energy of Münzer to increase the adherents of the revolutionary movement, and Münzer not unwillingly allowing himself to be guided by Pfeiffer's sagacity in matters of organisation, tactics, and the present ends to be striven for.

The expulsion occurred in September, 1524 and was accompanied by the exodus of many adherents of the movement. Münzer now entered upon a period of several weeks' travel, staying a short time in Nürnberg and then passing the winter in some part of south Germany. This tour, it has been, without doubt rightly, assumed, was of a propagandist character. Münzer certainly traversed various districts, possibly returning by way of Franconia. Pfeiffer, it is said, was back in Mühlhausen early in December, but it was certainly not before February, 1525, that Münzer again entered the gates of the imperial city. The powerful guild-following of Pfeiffer succeeded in effecting the latter's recall. This success led the adherents of Münzer in and around the town to agitate on behalf also of their leader. Foremost amongst these was an enthusiastic master of the skinners' guild, named Rothe, who, during his leader's absence, kept together the poor journeymen and city proletarians constituting the bulk of Münzer's following. On hearing the call of his disciples, Münzer hurried back to Thuringia. He was arrested on his way in the Fulda territory, but not being identified was released after a few days.

On his return, Münzer naturally found a strong opposition in the patrician party to his being allowed to preach, but his friends, who. had secured his re-admission to the city, reinforced by Pfeiffer's party, proved strong enough to overcome it. Münzer now began a vigorous agitation in the suburbs and the open country round the town. Presently, crowds flocked through the gates from the adjacent districts.

The council, alarmed, suddenly ordered the gates to be shut, but it was too late. The partisans of Münzer paraded the town at night, raising seditious cries and even demanding in menacing terms the death of certain prominent representatives of the old families and members of the council. The next day saw a most numerous exodus of the town patriciate.

Both Pfeiffer and Münzer had already established their position in the town, the one having taken possession of the Church of St. Nicholas and the other that of St. Mary. As town preachers they had insisted on the right of being present at all council meetings — a claim that the affrighted councillors durst not gainsay. A few of the patrician party, from either fear or conviction, now joined the popular government. An armed assembly of the citizens was called for the purpose of taking a muster roll. The opportunity was seized by Pfeiffer and Münzer to persuade the people to overthrow the existing council altogether. By an overwhelming majority the council was deposed.

The new council was nominated, with the consent of those assembled, by the burgher committee already spoken of, which Pfeiffer had instituted some months previously. It received the name of the "Eternal Council," a designation explained as implying that it should not, like its predecessor, be subject to a periodic renewal of a fourth of its members, but should continue to govern in its entirety until its mandate was formally revoked by the general assembly of the citizens. This explanation of the name is probably correct, but as the archives containing the constitution of this "Eternal Council" were destroyed in the events which followed, it is impossible now to determine its character precisely. The foregoing decisive stage in the Mühlhausen revolution was reached on the 17th of March, 1525. Pfeiffer and Münzer were henceforth practically dictators in their respective spheres, although they both remained in name merely the leading preachers of the two chief churches of the town. They attended all meetings of the new council, and important or doubtful points were, as a rule, referred to them to decide from the standpoint of the new religious doctrines. Pfeiffer probably exercised the greater influence within the town itself, whilst Münzer had the surrounding districts under his sway. Münzer endeavoured, moreover, it would seem, to keep in touch with the movements in other parts of Germany with which he had become acquainted in the course of his recent travels. His efforts in this direction were not crowned with any practical success, save in so far as Thuringia and the adjacent Hesse and Saxony were concerned.

Münzer now proceeded to put his communistic principles into practice on a small scale. The Johanniterhof, the foundation of the monks of St. John, was selected by him as a residence for himself and his chief disciples. The monks were turned out and the place reorganised on principles dictated by Münzer. Here the new religionists seemed to have lived in a manner after all not essentially different from that of a monastic order, — so true it is that the new, when it appears on the arena of history, almost uniformly adopts the garb of the old to which it opposes itself! Thus Christianity started first of all as a Jewish sect, and this it remained as long as its conscious opposition lay in Judaism. Later on, after it had spread throughout the Roman Empire, and after this opposition had been shifted to Paganism, it absorbed pagan doctrines, practices and rites wholesale, until in the final stage of the conflict in the fourth century there was little outwardly to distinguish the two.

To compare great things with small we find A similar phenomenon in the movement of English sectarian freethought, known as Secularism, which became popular some generations ago with some of the more intelligent of the lower middle and upper fringe of the working classes. This was supposed to be a protest against "church and chapel". Yet the moment it began to organise itself positively as a cult, it unconsciously had to adopt the forms of Nonconformist services. Turning to things economic, we find similarly the rising middle class holding fast to guild regulations and to various other relics of feudal times long after its opposition to the feudal classes had been emphasised by more. than one violent crisis. So it will probably be in the future. When new socialistic conditions of society take the place of present conditions, it will doubtless be found that for a time production and distribution of social wealth will be carried on upon lines little more than a development of the most advanced economic forms of modern capitalism.

There are in all new movements a Scylla and a Charybdis; the one consists in the mistaking the swaddling-clothes derived from the old as a part of the essential garb of the new, and the other consists in the premature and too drastic attempt to rid the new of these very swaddling-clothes. This applies to all changes, be they primarily religious, political, intellectual, aesthetic or economic. Thus the original Judaic Christianity was in time sloughed off as a heresy — the Eblonite heresy. On the opposite, the pagan side, the same thing happened with Gnosticism and Montanism. In modern Socialism again, have the state-socialistic tendency known in this country as Fabianism, which hugs old bureaucratic forms, and, on the other hand, we have the anarchistic tendency, which would abruptly abolish all existing administrative organisations.

Of course, it may be objected that Münzer's ideas were not new, that all medieval communistic theories issued in the long run in a species of monkery. This is true as far as the positive side of his teaching and action were concerned, but it must not be forgotten that the movements with which we are dealing, although on the positive side reactionary, as Lassalle justly pointed out, were on the negative side sufficiently in accord with the contemporary trend of social evolution. In fact, their failure definitely to break up the old feudal organisation contributed in a great measure to the backwardness of Germany for well-nigh three centuries, as compared with other countries of western Europe. Münzer's communism was still-born, but his antagonism to feudal and ecclesiastical privileges became common-places of the democratic thought of a later age. Again, his insistence on the paramount nature of the "inner light" was simply a mystical way of asserting the right of private judgment against tradition, and also the rights of the individual within his own sphere against external authority — ideas that have likewise become the theoretical cornerstones of post-medieval progressive movements. Outside the Johanniterhof, Münzer's communism at most extended itself to a distribution of corn and possibly other food-stuffs, and of pieces of cloth for the making of garments.

The new state of things attracted thousands of the country-folk into the town, where they were now gladly received. Münzer preached assiduously in the Marienkirche, and his sermons were followed by anthems sung by a choir of youths and maidens organised by himself, the words being taken from Old Testament exhortations and promises to the children of Israel.

The agitation, under Münzer's auspices, soon spread from Mühlhausen to the neighbouring territories, as far as Erfurt, Coburg, and even into the Hesse Duchy and the neighbourhood of Brunswick. At the beginning of April, the country was everywhere aflame. The archiepiscopal city of Erfurt itself was at one time besieged by bands of peasants some three or four thousand strong. They were induced to disperse by a harangue from the popular preacher Eberlin. Here, as elsewhere, noblemen were compelled to enter the peasant brotherhood, amongst them the Counts von Hohenstein. One of them narrowly escaped being lynched for a veiled threat uttered in response to an observation by one of the peasant leaders.

All this time Münzer remained in Mühlhausen, although he was in constant communication with his agents, notably with certain of them in the mining districts of the Mansfeld territories. He issued an address to the miners, exhorting them to hold together in the common cause, which was now everywhere in the ascendant. His activity within the city showed itself in the casting of cannon of heavy calibre, and in the holding of the forces together. Pfeiffer, on his side, occupied himself with organising and drilling his partisans.

It is a mistake to suppose that during the two months' régime of Münzer in Mühlhausen the whole town was animated by communistic sentiments. On the contrary, as Karl Kautsky has pointed out, Münzer's sect formed at most a tolerated imperium in impero, the fighting strength of which, judging by the number of those who went out with Münzer to the final battle, amounted to not more than some three hundred men. The close union with Pfeiffer and his movement was caused by the exigencies of the situation and the necessity for the complete overthrow of the patrician party in the town. Pfeiffer was almost exclusively interested in the success of the local revolt. Münzer, on the other hand, with his visions of a universal social revolution, was one of the few leaders in the Peasants War who attempted to bring unity, at least so far as Germany was concerned, into the insurrection, by establishing organised communication between the different centres. That he failed was due to the conditions already alluded to under which the movement arose, and not, as far as we can see, to any fault on his part. The whole movement was essentially local, and the materials for an effective centralisation were nowhere at hand.

Meanwhile, the princes, the Landgraf of Hesse and Duke George Henry of Brunswick, with other minor potentates, had collected their resources with a determination to make a definite end of the Thuringian revolt. The followers of Pfeiffer and Münzer within the walls of Mühlhausen seem to have got restive and to have forced the hands of their chiefs. That Münzer's hands were forced, if not Pfeiffer's, admits of no doubt. He seems to have been well aware that matters were not yet ripe, and that the artisans and peasants at the disposal of the insurrection were inadequate to meet the army of trained fighting men that the princes were preparing to hurl against them. Finally, Pfeiffer, either unable to keep his men in hand, or having become otherwise convinced of the necessity for action, compelled Münzer to join him in a sortie. In this sortie the usual booty was obtained, but no permanent results were achieved.

A few days later, Pfeiffer, on his part, remained inactive at Mühlhausen, when the situation urgently demanded an expedition for the relief of the main camp at Frankenhausen some miles away. The position of this camp was itself unwise. The correct policy would obviously have been for the whole available insurgent strength, to have entrenched itself in the well-fortified imperial city and to have used this as a base. Münzer in vain endeavoured to effectually arouse the Mansfelders, notwithstanding that Frankenhausen was in close proximity to the Mansfeld mines. The encamped peasants by the usual trickery were lured into negotiations with Count Albrecht until the arrival of the princes with their overwhelming force. Münzer joined the peasant bodies outside Frankenhausen on the 12th of May. Two days later, the Landgraf of Hesse with the Duke of Brunswick came within striking distance, and their strength was reinforced within twenty-four hours, by the arrival of the Duke of Saxony with a large and well-disciplined body of troops.

In point of numbers the two camps were now nearly equal, being composed of about eight thousand men each. But, in the one case, they were finely-equipped men-at-arms, well-supported by artillery, while, in the other case, they were inexperienced, badly-armed rustics and poor citizens, with only one or two pieces of ordnance in their midst. The insurgents were entrenched on an elevation a short distance from the town behind a stockade of waggons.

For information respecting the course of the battle, which took place on the 15th of May, the usual source is the highly-coloured and partisan narrative of Melancthon in his well-known pamphlet on Münzer and the Thuringian revolt. Melancthon puts a speech into the mouth of Münzer, in which he bids his followers to have no fear, for that God would deliver their enemies into their hands, and guarantees that the bullets should not hurt them, for that he himself would catch them in the sleeve of his mantle. This speech was followed, according to the same account, with one from the Landgraf Philip to his men, in the course of which he deprecated the aspersions cast by the insurgent leaders upon princes, nobles and the authorities generally. On the attack being thereupon made by the Landgraf's followers, it is stated that the peasants stood still singing the chorale, Nun bitten wir den Heiligen Geist (Now beseech we the Holy Ghost).

Another pamphlet, published the same year, 1525, implies that the princes and barons had given the insurgents a three hours' truce to consider their terms of surrender, but that having gained over the Count von Stolberg and some other nobles, who had hitherto been forced into siding with the peasants, they proceeded at once to the attack, thereby taking their adversaries by surprise. The latter account is unquestionably the more reliable of the two, since it coincides with the general treatment of the revolted peasants by their treacherous oppressors.

The following account of the battle is based upon Zimmermann (iii., pp.776-781), who had opportunities of consulting the Mühlhausen archives and other manuscript sources.

Münzer marched with his men to the elevation above Frankenhausen, called to this day the Schlachtberg. The negotiations entered into by the princes had had a demoralising effect upon the peasant army. A full amnesty was promised if they would only hand over their leaders, among whom Münzer was specially singled out. The noblemen who had been forced to join the peasants were naturally the most zealous advocates of surrender. On seeing themselves surrounded by the hostile ordnance, the peasant army sent the three Counts, von Stolberg, von Rixleben, and von Wertern, into the princely camp. This was the occasion of the three hours' truce already spoken of. Unconditional submission, with the surrender of Münzer, were the terms insisted upon. Two of the counts remained in the princely camp, and one returned to tell the tale. The party of surrender redoubled their efforts, a nobleman and a priest signalising themselves specially in their opposition to Münzer. The latter, still with his devoted bodyguard intact, and with a strong party amongst the other combatants, was able to cause the nobleman and priest to be beheaded. He then endeavoured to raise the enthusiasm of the camp by a discourse, denouncing the godless tyrants with more than his accustomed vehemence and adding allusions to Gideon, David, and other Biblical heroes, who with a small force of the chosen people had conquered hosts. This is the "bullet-catching" speech reported by Melancthon. He wound up, according to the same source, by pointing to a suddenly-appearing rainbow as a sign from heaven of their predestined triumph.

Whether the speech in question was genuine or was fabricated by Melancthon, the episode of the rainbow need not be doubted. In any case, Münzer succeeded in rousing his hearers to a momentary enthusiasm. They rejected the terms offered, and began to sing their hymn, the time of the truce not having yet expired. Suddenly the cannon of the princes thundered into the camp. Many looked upwards, says a contemporary manuscript quoted by Zimmermann, to behold whether help would not come from heaven. But before the legions of angels descended, the waggon-stockade was broken through, and "they were shot, pierced and miserably slain". In a few minutes the peasant army was dispersed and in full flight in various directions. A small body held its own for a short time in a stone quarry, only to be ultimately overpowered.

The bulk of the fugitives made for the town of Frankenhausen, hotly pursued by a detachment of the Landgraf's men-at-arms. Within the walls, the massacre was frightful, extending to churches, houses and monasteries, where refuge had been sought. The stream running through the chief street seemed turned to blood. More than five thousand peasants perished within a few hours, but, not yet satisfied, the princes had three hundred prisoners brought into the square before the Rathhaus to be beheaded, among them an old priest and his young assistant. The women of Frankenhausen begged for mercy for their husbands and brothers. This was accorded them on condition that they slew these two priests with their own hands.

According to the manuscript chronicle of Erfurt, "the Landgraf and Duke George delivered to the women a preacher and his assistant. They must perforce strike them dead with clubs, to the end that their husbands might remain in life. Therefore did the women in such wise beat them that their heads were like unto a rotten cabbage and the brains did cling unto the clubs. Thereupon were their husbands given unto them. The princes themselves did behold how this thing came to pass." The singling out of the clericals as scapegoats was obviously dictated by the feeling that they were in a special sense traitors to the cause of the governing classes.

Münzer, upon whose head a price had been set, and who was amongst the fugitives who reached Frankenhausen, fled into a deserted house hard by the gate. Concealing himself here in a loft, he threw off some of his clothes, and, binding his head with the hope of rendering himself unrecognisable lay down on a bed. A knight's servant, one of the pursuers, shortly afterwards entered the same house and discovered him in the loft. Münzer, whom he did not identify, pretended that he was ill of a fever, but the fellow's plundering instincts led him to search the knapsack lying near. He found therein correspondence that revealed the identity of the apparently sick man, and he straightway apprised his master of his valuable discovery.

Münzer was seized and brought before the princes, who asked him why he had misled the poor people. He had done what he had done, he replied, because the princes persecuted the Gospel and sacrificed all to their avarice and lusts. The young Landgraf then admonished him with the well-known quotations from Holy Writ as to the duty of obeying authority, to which admonitions Münzer made no reply. Thereupon he was handed over to the executioner to be tortured. In the midst of his suffering, on being once more reproached with having led his followers to destruction, he said with a grim smile, "They would not have it otherwise," apparently referring to the premature action of the insurgents.

He was subsequently sent to his arch-enemy, Count Ernst von Mansfeld, who immured him in a dungeon in the tower at Heldrungen. Here he dictated his celebrated letter to the inhabitants of Mühlhausen, in which he certainly "backs down". So much must be said in spite of the attempt of Zimmermann and other admirers of Münzer to give the letter a more favourable interpretation. He not merely deprecates any further attempts at insurrection, advice that might be dictated by the hopelessness of the situation, but confesses to having "seductively and rebelliously preached many opinions, delusions and errors concerning the Holy Sacrament . . . as also against the ordinances of the universal Christian Church". Further, he confesses himself as dying as "a once again reconciled member of the Holy Christian Church," praying God to forgive him his former conduct. The only redeeming passage is one that pleads for his wife and child, that they might not be deprived of his worldly goods.

The doubts suggested by Kautsky as to the genuineness of this letter are hardly tenable. It may have been to the interest of the princes that such a letter should have been written, and they may have terrorised him into writing it, in the same way as prison authorities may from time to time have terrorised innocent persons condemned to death into "confessing" and acknowledging the justice of their sentence". But when Kautsky endeavours to impugn its having issued from Münzer by asking why he dictated it instead of writing it, the answer is sufficiently clear. A man who had so recently suffered the last extremities of the thumbscrew would hardly be able to write autograph letters.

The scandalous lack of solidarity among the peasants is particularly illustrated in this Thuringian revolt. Two important armed bodies which might well have turned the scale, heavy weighted as it was on the side of the nobles, were carousing not many miles away, when they ought to have been hastening to the assistance of their brethren at Frankenhausen.

Pfeiffer's party in Mühlhausen. on the 19th of May, wrote a despairing letter to the Franconian insurgents, apprising them of the destruction of the Frankenhausen force and imploring them to come to their assistance. But it was of no avail. They had their own dissensions and their own local objects, with but little feeling for the general movement.

Meanwhile Münzer was taken from the tower at Heldrungen and brought for execution into the camp of the princes, which now lay before Mühlhausen itself. The imperial city was surrounded on three sides. Pfeiffer, who commanded in the town, was, in face of the imminent danger, beginning to lose his popularity. The demand for the unconditional surrender of the ringleaders, and especially of Pfeiffer, became increasingly favoured by the citizens. As breaches were made in the walls and the position seemed more and more hopeless, notwithstanding the heroic defence of Pfeiffer's twelve hundred faithful followers, the public sentiment in favour of capitulation quickly gained the upper hand. Finally, on the 24th of May, seeing that all was lost, Pfeiffer escaped from the town with four hundred adherents, with the object of joining the Franconian insurgents.

The next day twelve hundred Mühlhausen women, with tattered clothes, bare feet and dishevelled hair, and five hundred virgins with mourning wreaths, streamed out of the gate leading to the princes' camp, where they presented themselves to implore mercy for their native city. They were given bread and cheese, but were informed that the men themselves of the town must put in an appearance. This was done. A number of prominent citizens came, bareheaded and barefooted, with white staves in their hands, and kneeling three times before the assembled princes handed over the keys of the town. After the combined army had made its entry the citizens were compelled to deliver up their arms. The "Eternal Council" set up by Pfeiffer and Münzer was deposed, and the old patrician council reinstated. Executions followed, that of the bürgermeister amongst them. The chief fortifications were levelled with the ground. The imperial city was deprived of its freedom, and reduced to the status of a tribute-paying town. Weapons, treasure, horses were seized, and it was only spared a wholesale sacking by a ransom of 40,000 gulden.

On learning of Pfeiffer's flight, the princes sent a body of horsemen in pursuit. They came up with his party near Eisenach, where, after a desperate resistance, Pfeiffer was taken with ninety-two of his men and brought back bound into the camp. They were all, or nearly all, instantly condemned to death and executed together, Pfeiffer scorning confession and sacrament, and dying without sign of fear or wavering. These facts regarding Pfeiffer are admitted even by his enemies.

Münzer, on the other hand, is accused by the same chroniclers of having shown up to the last a spirit of faltering and pusillanimity which, it must be admitted, accords with the tone of his Heldrungen letter. The badgering of their victim by the princes was significant. The Catholic Duke George of Saxony admonished him to repent of having forsaken his order and of having taken a wife. The young Lutheran Landgraf of Hesse told him that he had no need to repent of these things, but that what he had to repent of was his having led the people into rebellion. Münzer, in his turn, admitted that he had attempted matters beyond his powers, but urgently entreated the princes and nobles to deal more mercifully with their subjects, and to read diligently the Holy Scriptures, especially the books of Samuel and the Kings, and to take to heart the lesson, there related, as to the miserable end of tyrants.

After this speech he said no more, as he was awaiting the stroke of the executioner. He did not even break his silence on being challenged to recite the "Credo," owing, as his enemies allege, to the extremity of his fear, or, as his friends suggest, to his contempt of the conventional usage. His head was struck off, and was fixed upon a long pole, as also was that of Pfeiffer, and his body was impaled.

After the defeat at Frankenhausen, and the surrender of Mühlhausen, the suppression of the revolt throughout the rest of Thuringia offered no great difficulty, and was largely effected by the individual princes and lords, each in his own territory. The plunder and devastation by the insurgents had not been less in Thuringia than elsewhere. As many as forty-six castles and monasteries lay in ruins. In the chief places the usual bloodthirsty executions followed. In Erfurt the old council was restored to office, and proceeded with merciless severity against all connected with the recent risings.

The battle of Frankenhausen is a landmark in the history of the Peasants War, and was synchronous within a few days with crushing defeats of the insurgents in other parts of Germany. The insurrection, which up to the beginning of May had, speaking generally, carried all before it, by that time had reached the turning-point, and its fortunes henceforward as steadily receded. In our next chapter we shall follow the disasters and the final extinction of the various movements, the rise and temporary success of which we have been describing.

Chapter VIII. The Suppression of the Insurrection throughout Germany.

It is now time to consider the attitude of Luther Throughout the crisis. His action was mainly embodied in two documents, of which the first was issued about the middle of April, and the second a month later. The difference in tone between them is sufficiently striking. In the first, which bore the title, "An Exhortation to Peace on the Twelve Articles of the Peasantry in Swabia," Luther sits on the fence, admonishing both parties of what he deemed their shortcomings. He was naturally pleased with those articles that demanded the free preaching of the Gospel and abused the Catholic clergy, and was not indisposed to assent to many of the economic demands. In fact, the document strikes one as distinctly more favourable to the insurgents than to their opponents.

"We have," he wrote, "no one to thank for its mischief and sedition, save ye princes and lords, in especial ye blind bishops and mad priests and monks, who up to this day remain obstinate and do not cease to rage and rave against the holy Gospel, albeit ye know that it is righteous, and that ye may not gainsay it. Moreover, in your worldly regiment, ye do naught otherwise than flay and extort tribute, that ye may satisfy your pomp and vanity, till the poor, common man cannot, and may not, bear with it longer. The sword is on your neck. Ye think ye sit so strongly in your seats, that none may cast you from them. Such presumption and obstinate pride will twist your necks, as ye will see." And again: "God hath made it thus that they cannot, and will not longer bear with your raging. If ye do it not of your free will, so shall ye be made to do it by way of violence and undoing." Once more: "It is not peasants, my dear lords, who have set themselves up against you. God Himself it is who setteth Himself against you to chastise your evil-doing."

He counsels the princes and lords to make peace with their peasants, observing with reference to the Twelve Articles, that some of them are so just and righteous, that before God and the world their worthiness is manifested, making good the words of the psalm that they heap contempt upon the heads of the princes. Whilst he warns the peasants against sedition and rebellion, and criticises some of the Articles as going beyond the justification of Holy Writ, and whilst he makes side-hits at "the prophets of murder and the spirits of confusion which had found their way among them," the general impression given by the pamphlet is, as already said, one of unmistakable friendliness to the peasants and hostility to the lords.

The manifesto may be summed up in the following terms: Both sides are, strictly speaking, in the wrong, but the princes and lords have provoked the "common man" by their unjust exactions and oppressions; the peasants, on their side, have gone too far in many of their demands, notably in the refusal to pay tithes, and most of all in the notion of abolishing villeinage, which Luther declares to be "straight-away contrary to the Gospel and thievish ". The great sin of the princes remains, however, that of having thrown stumbling-blocks in the r .way of the Gospel- bien entendu the Gospel according to Luther — and the main virtue of the peasants was their claim to have this Gospel preached. It call scarcely be doubted that the ambiguous tone of Luther's rescript was interpreted by the rebellious peasants to their advantage and served to stimulate, rather than to check, the insurrection.

Meanwhile, the movement rose higher and higher, and reached Thuringia, the district with which Luther personally was most associated. His patron, and what is more, the only friend of toleration in high places, the noble-minded Elector Friedrich of Saxony, fell ill and died on the 5th of May, and was succeeded by his younger brother Johann, the same who afterwards assisted in the suppression of the Thuringian revolt. Almost immediately thereupon, Luther, who had been visiting his native town of Eisleben, travelled through the revolted districts on his way back to Wittenberg. He everywhere encountered black looks and jeers. When he preached, the Münzerites would drown his voice by the ringing of bells. The signs of rebellion greeted him on all sides. The "Twelve Articles" were constantly thrown at his head. As the reports of violence towards the property and persons of some of his own noble friends reached him, his rage broke all bounds. He seems, however, to have prudently waited a few days, until the cause of the peasants was obviously hopeless, before publicly taking his stand on the side of the authorities.

On his arrival in Wittenberg, he wrote a second pronouncement on the contemporary events, in which no uncertainty was left as to his attitude. It is entitled, "Against the Murderous and Thievish Bands of Peasants".(1) Here he lets himself loose on the side of the oppressors with a bestial ferocity. "Crush them the peasants," he writes, "strangle them and pierce them, in secret places and in sight of men, he who can, even as one would strike dead a mad dog." All having authority who hesitated to extirpate the insurgents to the uttermost were committing a sin against God. "Findest thou thy death therein," he writes, addressing the reader, "happy art thou; a more blessed death can never overtake thee, for thou diest in obedience to the Divine word and the command of Romans xiii. 1, and in the service of love, to save thy neighbour from the bonds of hell and the devil." Never had there been such an infamous exhortation to the most dastardly murder on a wholesale scale since the Albigensian crusade with its "Strike them all; God will know His own" — a sentiment indeed that Luther almost literally reproduces in one passage.

Many efforts have been made by Protestant historians to palliate this crime of Luther's, more especially to shield him against the charge of time-serving and cowardice in adopting an attitude of benevolent neutrality to the peasants' cause at a time when it bade fair to be successful, whilst hounding on its executioners to hideous barbarities when its prospects were obviously desperate. One of the more recent of these Protestant writers, Egelhaaf (Deutsche Geschichte im sechszehnten Jahrhundert, vol. i., p.614), endeavours to establish the probability that Luther issued this pamphlet a day or two before the catastrophe at Frankenhausen, or at least before he could have known of the peasants' overthrow in Würtemberg. Even if this were true, which is hardly probable, it would not help Luther's character, for, from his immediate personal knowledge of the situation in Thuringia, he must have seen, at least from the beginning of the second week in May, that the forces of the combined princes, with their trained men-at-arms and adequate supply of artillery, were destined to win against bands of peasants and handicraftsmen, ill-armed, unused to fighting, and insufficiently munitioned. As for the other districts, a report could hardly have failed to reach him concerning the demoralisation of the peasant armies and the reinforcement of the Swabian League's strength with knights and free-lances returned from the Italian campaign. Altogether, this second manifesto remains an ineffaceable stigma upon the powerful personality of the "rebellious monk" of Wittenberg.

We turn now again to the fortunes of Truchsess and the overthrow of the movement in south Germany. The force of the Swabian League, under Truchsess, by the armistice or treaty at Weingarten, made with the three combined contingents of the Swabian insurgents, known respectively as the Ried, the Lake, and the Algau contingents, was saved, as Zimmermann has pointed out, from imminent disaster — since the insurgents not only considerably, outnumbered the troops of imperial order, but were well supplied with ordnance captured from sundry castles, and occupied a strong position. The utter fecklessness of the counsels of the insurrection was never more exemplified than in the feeble surrender of all these advantages to the blandishments of Truchsess. At this time, Truchsess was practically hemmed in, but, on the dispersal of the greater part of the country-folk arrayed against him, he was at once extricated from a difficult situation, and had his hands left free to move southwards, destroying or scattering bodies of peasants on the way.

He took this direction with a view of attacking the Black Forest contingent. which was now making itself very active, especially in the siege of Radolfzell with its refugee nobles. On the 25th of April, he was met by a deputation of the Hegau and Black Forest insurgents for the purpose of negotiations. A similar arrangement to the one mentioned was attempted but failed. On the emissaries returning to their respective contingents, Truchsess continued his march to Stockach, and finally pitched his camp a short distance from the important fortress of Duke Ulrich, the Hohentwiel. His further movements in this neighbourhood were stopped by the peremptory order from the Council of the Swabian League at Ulm that he was to proceed straight to the relief of Würtemberg. Unwillingly giving up his plans in the south, he returned by forced marches to his old camp on the Neckar.

Meanwhile, on the 7th of May, some cavalry of the Markgraf Kasimir von Ansbach, strengthened by a force sent by the Count Palatine from the Upper Palatinate, attacked a large body of peasants, who had just captured the small town of Wettingen. They had come from plundering a neighbouring monastery, and were marching in great disorder, intent in the main apparently upon carrying off their heavily-laden waggons of booty. The onslaught was sudden and unexpected, and resulted in the slaughter, almost without resistance, of over a thousand peasants. This was the first serious check inflicted by the princely power upon the movement in south Germany since the Leipheim affair; but the decisive battle was fought on May 12th, when the united forces under Truchsess, consisting of 6000 free-lances and 1,200 horse, met the main body of the peasant army of Würtemberg, 12,000 strong, between the towns of Böblingen and Sindelfingen. Ritter Bernhardt von Winterstetten was the commander of this section, Matern Feuerbacher, owing to his moderate tendencies and general indecision, having been deposed.

Truchsess succeeded, by the aid of treachery on the part of some of the leading citizens of Böblingen, who opened their gates to his men, in throwing a detachment into the castle above the town. From this point of vantage he opened fire upon the insurgents, who were entrenched in a strong position behind some marshy ground, compelling them ultimately to gain the open. No sooner was this the case than the horse of the Palatinate and of the Austrians attacked them in front, whilst four companies of foot opened fire on their flank. The battle, which began at ten in the morning, lasted four hours. By two o'clock the flight general. The fugitives were hotly pursued, and for seven or eight miles the way was strewed with the corpses of peasants cut down the horsemen of the princes' army. The counts of the numbers slain vary between two thousand and six thousand. The whole of the peasants' ordnance, thirty-three pieces, fell into the hands of the League.

Amongst the prisoners captured after the battle was Melchior Nonnenmacher, Helfenstein's former piper, who, it will be remembered, had taken so prominent a part in the execution of his master and the other knights outside the walls of Weinsberg. With savage ferocity, Truchsess, the same evening, had him bound by chains to an apple-tree, his tether allowing m a run of two paces, and then, faggots having been heaped up in a circle round, they were set alight and the wretched piper was slowly roasted to death.

The victorious League and its allies swept trough the villages and small towns of Würtemberg, plundering, burning and slaying. At every halt made executions took place, hangings or beheadings. Neckarsulm and Oehringen were bombarded and surrendered. Weinsberg was reserved for a heavy vengeance; its few remaining inhabitants were driven out, with the exception of one or two who refused to go, and who therefore perished, and the town itself with all it contained was burned to the ground. By order of Truchsess, in the name of the League, it was forbidden to be rebuilt, and it remained for some years a witness of princely vindictiveness. Poor Jäcklein Rohrbach, endeavouring in vain to rally a few defenders of the people's cause, was recognised as he was passing through a village, and delivered over to Truchsess. He met a similar fate to that of Nonnenmacher, being, it is stated, chained to an elm-tree and roasted alive, whilst the assembled princes and nobles gloated over his agony.

Meanwhile the Count Palatine had taken the town of Bruchsal and hewn off nine heads there. Truchsess proceeded against Wimpfen, sending a messenger to demand the surrender of the leaders of the movement in that town. The council, with some unwillingness, consented to the arrest of certain persons. The Counts of Hohenlohe, who, it will be remembered, had had to make a pact with the peasants, were visited by Truchsess, and compelled to swear never again to have aught to do with the malcontents. One of the Weinsberg rebels was caught in the town of Oehringen and hanged on a tree.

Würtemberg was thus effectively subdued. The property of Hans Flux in Heilbronn was made over by Truchsess to the executioner who accompanied him throughout his campaign, and whose truculence was even a little much for the not too sensitive councillors of the Swabian League at Ulm. This ruffian, however, was safe in the sunshine of the favour and protection of his master, who called him his "dear Berthold".

The peasant council in Heilbronn, of which Wendel Hipler was the presiding genius, hastily dispersed and fled before the approach Truchsess. Hipler himself hurried back to the camp at Würzburg. At the end of May Truchsess combined his forces with those of Count Palatine Ludwig, by which step the League's strength was increased by two thousand foot, twelve hundred horse and fourteen large pieces of ordnance. The Archbishop of Trier and the Bishop of Würzburg, with other territorial magnates, subsequently joined hands with Truchsess, with the ultimate object of relieving the Frauenberg and the town of Würzburg, where, as we have already seen, the main army of the insurrection in central Germany was massed.

Although the backbone of the movement in Würtemberg was broken by the recent victories of the League and its allies, the insurrection elsewhere, as, for instance, in the Black Forest and in Breisgau, not to speak of the hereditary Austrian dominions, was still maintaining itself with unabated vigour. Hans Müller von Bulgenbach was threatening all who did not join his Christian Brotherhood with the worldly ban, in modern phraseology a universal "boycott," which forbade men to eat or drink with them, to work in their company, to offer them food, drink, salt, or wood, and to buy or sell with them. Freiburg, Breisach and Waldkirch were with difficulty holding out against the bodies of peasants by which they were being pressed. The town of Villingen was especially in a bad way. But the destruction of the great Franconian peasant army at Würzburg, and above all the relief of the Frauenberg, which it was feared would have to surrender in a few days, were undoubtedly of first importance at the moment to the League and its allies. The capture of the strong fortress that commanded the episcopal city would have given the insurrection a point d'appui in the very heart of Germany, and although, as already remarked, the possible gain was certainly not worth the locking up of such an enormous mass of the peasant forces in one place, its significance for the popular movement cannot be denied.

The successes of the princely power in Würtemberg had the effect of strengthening the Würzburg camp, which had. thus become a rallying point , whither fragments of dispersed contingents and companies of peasants hurriedly took their way. It will be remembered that on 5th of May, the same day, that is, as that on which the defeat at Frankenhausen took place and only three days after the overthrow at Böblingen, the besiegers had unsuccessfully stormed the aforesaid Würzburg castle of the Marienburg. This failure, as we know, led to recriminations between the army and its leaders, Götz being specially singled out for suspicion of treachery. In the end, however, a council of war was held, and Götz was sent with a detachment of eight thousand men to endeavour to prevent the union of the Palatinate force with that of the League under Truchsess, of which project news had already arrived. All along, according to his own account, Götz had been acting from compulsion, and under present circumstances we may well believe that he wished nothing better than to shake off his responsibilities at the earliest opportunity. Thus it happened that one dark night he disappeared, afterwards salving his conscience for this seeming treachery with the excuse that the four weeks for which he had pledged himself to act as peasant commander had expired.

On his escape becoming known, about a fourth part of his men deserted to their homes. The remainder moved onwards in a body to Königshofen on the Tauber. Here, some six thousand in number, they solemnly swore to be avenged upon Truchsess, the League, and the Princes. On the 2nd of June the combined forces of the nobles reached Königshofen, passing over the Tauber at a place feebly defended by the peasants. The camp was attacked, and soon the whole contingent was confused flight, leaving its stockade of waggons and its ordnance a prey to the enemy, who soon held complete possession of the elevation on which the camp had stood. Only about one thousand succeeded in rallying and entrenching themselves in a neighbouring wood where, quickly improvising a stockade of trees and bushes, they succeeded in holding out for a short time. Their stockade, however, was ultimately broken through, and five hundred were speared on the spot, shot from trees, or trampled down by the horsemen. More than two thousand had already fallen in the original encounter. Most of the leaders are stated to have escaped on the backs of the horses taken from the ammunition waggons. Truchsess was wounded in the hip by a lance.

The defeat at Königshofen was for the peasants little less serious than those at Böblingen and Frankenhausen. The main force, is true, was still at Würzburg. Other divisions, however, had detached themselves with the view of checking the League's advance. At this moment some of Truchsess's mercenaries demanded their battle-pay, notwithstanding that they had not been among those actively engaged in the encounter. A serious mutiny seemed inevitable, and thus a gleam of hope showed itself for the peasants. Enough men, however, including the military leaders, remained to save the situation for the League.

Florian Geyer, with his "Black Troop," to which were joined several other peasant companies, now broke from the camp at Würzburg with the intention of intercepting the princely forces on the road to that city. He and his men, furious at the reports that reached them of burning villages and of peasants strung up on every tree, the traces left of the victorious march of Truchsess and his allies, avowed that they would hang every knight and cut the throat of every free-lance. Meanwhile, the bulk of Truchsess's mutinous mercenaries had caught him up and returned to their allegiance. Truchsess, who would gladly have punished them, was nevertheless compelled by the exigencies of the situation to pardon and reinstate them.

Florian Geyer, with his troop, appears to have had no certain information respecting the battle of Königshofen and still believed that the camp of his friends lay between himself and the allied princes. Accompanied by a few horsemen, Florian was riding in front, below the castle of Ingolstatt, when the advancing body of peasants found themselves suddenly surrounded and attacked by the whole force of the enemy. Taken unawares, they had scarcely time to get their ordnance into position or to bring their train of waggons properly into a stockade. With the presence of mind of a trained fighting man, however, Florian at once rallied all his companies into some sort of battle array, improvising a rough stockade and immediately beginning a fire from such artillery as he had. But in a few minutes it was only too evident that his force was outmatched. The attack of the free-lances was supported by the entire body of horsemen, but the signal for flight seems to have been given by the sudden and simultaneous thunder of all the enemy's heavy ordnance, which had just been brought to the other side of the stockade. The panic was immediate and general. Dispersed in their mad flight, the insurgents were ridden down, run down, or clubbed to death. For miles around the slaughter extended. Sixty who were taken alive, from whom some of the free-lances wished to extract ransom-money, were ordered by Truchsess to be butchered in a heap.

A remnant of the "Black Troop" alone held together, and with Florian at their head, some six hundred in number, succeeded in reaching the village of Ingolstatt. Having entrenched themselves behind a hedge stockade, they awaited the onslaught of the Count Palatine Ludwig, who advanced against them at the head of twelve hundred knights. Two hundred of the troopers occupied the churchyard and the church, whilst more than three hundred seized upon the castle above the village. Here a continuous fire was kept up, to which was added the hurling down of tiles and pieces of the wall. The attacking party flung fire brands into the church, which after some time blazed up, all the defenders being destroyed.

The last defence was the castle, already partly in ruins from an attack of the peasants some weeks previously. Florian himself commanded the brave band within. They barricaded the gates and breaches so effectively that the stormers were held in check for a long while, besides being repeatedly driven back by the hail of bullets that rained from every opening. Soon the whole army of the enemy, which had meanwhile come up, was engaged exclusively in the attack on this stronghold, but the thick wall of the old feudal fortress did not yield until all the strength of Truchsess's cannon had been brought to bear upon it. Dismounting, knights and barons struggled together with the free-lances for an entrance at the breach made. More than a hundred of the storming contingent lay killed and wounded in the fosse below, and still the attack seemed no nearer success. Finally, a last effort was about to be made, when suddenly the firing from within ceased; the defenders had exhausted their ammunition. Resistance was still kept up with tiles and stones. Even on an entrance being effected, a hand-to-hand fight ensued. The besieged neither asked nor obtained quarter. At last, fifty of them withdrew fighting into the deep cellars, whilst from amid the mass of dead surrounding them, about two hundred of the "Black Troop," led by Florian, succeeded in escaping under cover of the approaching darkness, just as the allied forces poured into the heap of ruins, which was now all that was left above ground of the ancient castle of Ingolstatt.

The two hundred entrenched themselves in a wood hard by, whence at intervals they made sorties. With daylight, the men of Truchsess burst into the wood, slaughtering all who remained there. But even now the valiant knight was not amongst the dead. With a few who were prepared to follow him to the death, he had towards morning struck out into the open country. All the neighbouring villages were set on fire by Truchsess's men, and all the inhabitants who were not consumed were, put to the sword. Amongst these villages was Giebelstatt, the castle above which was Florian's hereditary home. His ultimate aim was, probably, to reach Würzburg. In the neighbouring territories far and wide all the companies, including the great Gailsdorf contingent, seven thousand strong, which had as yet suffered no great losses, were dispersed. Alarmed by the accounts of the disasters of Königshofen and Ingolstatt, their members had fled into the woods or had returned to their homes and again done homage to their feudal lords.

It is doubtful whether Florian Geyer ever again saw Würzburg. After a few days' wandering in company with a handful of followers, during which days he had reached, as the old account alleges, the Hall territory far to the south, he and his men are said to have been surprised by a detachment of horsemen led by the brother of his betrothed, Wilhelm von Grumbach. A fierce, desperate struggle ensued, in the course of which the chivalrous hero of the people's cause fell fighting.(2) Recent researches have pointed to the probability that family disputes, or jealousies, played their part in the death of Geyer. His name has ever since been cherished in Germany by the lovers of freedom, and his personality has always been surrounded by the nimbus of popular fancy, as that of the ideal hero of revolt against oppression. For centuries after, legend related how the figure of his bride was to be seen flitting through the moonlit glades in the neighbourhood of her ancestral castle.

After these bloody conflicts, Truchsess had to make a roll-call of the forces of the Swabian League under his command. His losses had been considerable, a fourth of the then having perished in several companies. The losses of his allies can hardly have been less. The march on Würzburg could now be undertaken without danger of serious resistance. On the evening of Whit Monday, the 5th of June, the outlying township of Heidingsfeld was reached, and here the princely army pitched its camp, the ordnance being pointed against the city. There were still, however, from five to six thousand peasants and burghers under arms, determined on defence, within the walls.

Meanwhile the bürgermeister and the members of the old city council placed themselves in negotiation with Truchsess with a view of betraying the city together with the insurgent leaders. They came to a secret understanding with Truchsess and the Count Palatine, by which the town was to pay a heavy ransom to the latter and to the bishop. The citizens were to be disarmed. Allegiance to the bishop was to be resworn under the old conditions, and last, but not least, the chiefs of the peasant army still within the town were to be surrendered. At the same time the bürgermeister and council pretended to the defenders that all they had done had been to negotiate favourable terms with the conquering host now before the walls, further resistance being represented by them as hopeless. The deception did its work, and on the morning of the 8th of June, Truchsess and the princes entered Würzburg in triumph, followed by fifteen hundred men-at-arms. The citizens were ordered to present themselves on the market-place. Those from the smaller country towns in the neighbourhood and the peasants were to appear at two other points respectively. All three places were afterwards surrounded by armed men. Truchsess then appeared on horseback, accompanied by four executioners with drawn swords. After admonishing the crowd on their crime of disobedience and declaring their lives all forfeit, while the assembled citizens with bared heads knelt before him, he retired with the princes into the Rathhaus and deliberated for more than an hour. On returning, sentences were delivered and the executions began. The heads of the principal leaders of the town-democracy fell.

Truchsess and his executioners then betook themselves to the open space where the companies furnished by the neighbouring small towns were assembled. Their leaders, to the number of twenty-four, were beheaded. The conquerors then went to the ditch whither the peasants had been summoned. Thirty-seven of the latter were singled out for death, to gratify the blood-lust of their baronial enemies.

Altogether, eighty-one executions took place within the town on this day. Amongst them was that of a peasant who had not been called, but who had pushed his way to the front to see how it fared with his comrades. He was seized by the executioner and beheaded with the others. As for the rank and file, their arms and armour had been already surrendered. Staves were now placed in their hands and they were driven from the town. Of these, many were slain on their way home by the brutal free-lances, who were prowling about. The town had to pay 8,000 gulden to the Swabian League, whilst the bishop with his clergy, together with the nobles who had held fiefs of him, subsequently received more than 200,000 gulden.

With the capture of the town of Würzburg was involved the relief of its citadel, the Marienburg, on the Frauenberg. When the conquerors entered it, the extent of the damage done to this powerful fortress by the peasant attack seems to have created surprise. Hans Lutz, the herald of Truchsess, observes in his diary: "Afterwards beheld I the castle at Würzburg, which was altogether shot through, together with the outer wall, which had a breach in it six klafters wide, and the peasants had made two ditches on the hill such as no man might believe. Moreover, had they brought up on the hill more than an hundred ladders and had made a ditch above the church called that of Saint Burckhardt, the which I have measured and did number an hundred and eighteen steps from the beginning of the ditch." He further adds the detail that "the peasants in this same church had smote off the heads of all the saints and of our Lord also".

The idea of the peasants seems to have been to blow up the castle, and to this end trains were apparently laid from the fosse in question. The besieged, whose provisions and ammunition were running low, had been apprised by Truchsess by certain signs, probably by beacon fires, of his approach. In consequence they did not spare powder and shot, but at once opened a heavy fire upon the town. It is probable that this, combined with the intelligence of the victories in the proximity, of the army of the allied princes, had its psychological effect in cowing the inhabitants of the town, including the peasant contingents, and in inducing them to consent to surrender rather than to insist on holding out to the last.

For eight days the "terror" in the surrounding districts lasted. Amongst the plundering and murdering princes and barons, the Markgraf Kasimir specially signalised himself. Promises of mercy were treacherously and wantonly broken. Executions took place everywhere, whilst those who did not suffer by the headsman, or the hangman, had their hands or their fingers hacked off, or their eyes pierced out. To the latter victims the Markgraf observed: "Ye swore ye would not see me again, and I will look to it that ye shall not break your oath". It was forbidden under severe penalties to shelter, to lead, or to heal them. Many died, and others were seen long afterwards wandering as beggars on the highway. For miles around the free-lances continued to plunder and burn the villages. Heavy ransoms were laid upon all districts. In the country they were usually reckoned at so much per hearth, whilst the towns paid as a rule en bloc. In Nordlingen, and other places which had not collectively taken an active part in the rebellion, only suspect citizens had to pay ransom money. The Markgraf Kasimir alone extracted 200,000 gulden within the next two years from his own subjects.

The free imperial town of Rothenburg was taken by Kasimir on the 28th of June. The populace had quite lost head and heart. A few of the leaders in this case, however, succeeded in escaping. Karlstadt was let down one night by a rope from a window in a house on the town wall, and ended his days as a respectable professor of theology in the Basel University. The Commenthur Christen also managed to flee to a safe place, as did Ehrenfried Kumpf, the old iconoclastic bürgermeister. On the other hand, Menzinger, Deuschlin, and the blind monk Schmidt, with other preachers of the new doctrine and popular leaders, met their deaths at the hands of Kasimir and the vengeful patricians now again in office. The latter indeed continued, after Kasimir and his men had left, to wreak vengeance upon their victims, slaying, branding and scourging without mercy, levelling houses to the ground and confiscating goods.

In the northern part of the Duchy of Franconia, the prince-bishop of Würzburg, the prince-coadjutor of Fulda and the old Count Henneberg, who, it will be remembered, had been forced some weeks previously to join the peasant brotherhood, raged from end to end of the district, revoking charters, taking ransoms, beheading for the pleasure of it, and enjoying the spectacle with their boon companions over their cups. The bishopric of Bamberg had been subdued without any difficulty by Truchsess after he left Wiirzburg. The usual executions followed. Here also houses were destroyed, and the ransom of 170,000 gulden was exacted for the bishop and his noble feudatories.

In the towns of the Rhenish district the revolt collapsed almost of itself. Mainz again did homage. Speyer made up its account with its bishop. Worms returned to its allegiance. Frankfurt-am-Main, however, whither many fugitives of the people's cause had come for refuge, was not visited by the soldiery of the princes, the council having succeeded by bribes in getting the town spared. Meanwhile the guilds and the popular party here, alarmed by the events occurring outside, had made terms with the council, or, rather, had dropped their original demands. Truchsess had turned his steps in the direction of Upper Swabia, where the insurrection had, as yet, not been crushed. Here also the peasants were destined to undergo a similar fate to that of their brethren in other parts of Germany.

Memmingen, the town where the peasants' parliament had been held in the early days of the revolt, and where the "Twelve Articles" were first adopted and probably drawn up, fell, as others had done, through treachery. The party of the Ehrbarkeit and certain councillors held secret communications with the Swabian League. On the Friday of Whitsun week the watchman announced to the council that a vast force of soldiery was bearing down upon the town. The citizens were instantly aroused, and the market-place glittered with armour and halberds. But on the leaders of the approaching force reaching the town; they merely asked with fair words for quarters for one hundred horsemen, the rest of their following to remain outside. This was eventually agreed to, and the citizens, imagining all danger over, laid down their arms and went home. No sooner were they out of the way than the League's men suddenly forced open the gates, and admitted their fellows from outside the walls to the number of two hundred horse and two thousand foot. Several citizens compromised in the recent rising immediately fled, among them the supposed author of the "Twelve Articles," the preacher Schappeler, who succeeded in reaching his native town of St. Gallon in safety. Five who remained were beheaded on the marketplace.

The Archduke Friedrich, who was anxious to get the territory of Upper Swabia as a fief of the House of Austria, and who had been negotiating to this end with the Algau insurgents, wished to prevent Truchsess, at all events for the moment, from carrying hostilities into this region, and wrote to Truchsess to this effect. The latter communicated with Ulm on the matter, but was told by the council of the League that he was acting in their service and not in that of the Archduke Friedrich, and that he was to proceed without delay. He obeyed, but seems to have been rather nettled by the peremptory language, since a short time afterwards, on the council's remonstrating with him for his wholesale burning of villages and homesteads, he sent back a reply that if they were going to teach him how to carry on war they had better come out and take the command themselves, and he would sit quiet at Kempten.

A portion of the Algau peasant army, on the approach of Truchsess, withdrew after a short skirmish to the other side of the river Luibas, and took up their position on a steep elevation, first destroying the ford. Here messengers were sent to call up the whole of the Algau forces. They had good and sufficient ordnance. The Algau peasants enjoyed the reputation, which seems to have been well founded, of being the best and most practised fighting men amongst the country population. Many of them had already served as freelances, and a considerable body of men-at-arms, recently back from the Italian war, had joined them. Walter Bach, before spoken of, who had once been in the Austrian service, and Kaspar Schneider, who had served in Italy under the well-known Georg von Frundsberg, were amongst their leaders. In a few days their number had risen to 23,000, one of the largest masses the peasants ever succeeded in bringing together to any one place.

The insurgents never had a more favourable opportunity. Had they succeeded in crushing Truchsess, as they could easily have done, Ethe cause of the rebellion might still, even now, have been saved. But where mischance or superior fighting strength did not destroy the peasants, treachery came in to do the work. Walter Bach opened negotiations with the head of the League's forces, under whom at an earlier period he had served. Truchsess was awaiting the advent of Georg von Frundsberg, who was on his way to reinforce him with three thousand free-lances. These had all fought under him at the battle of Pavia.

It was on the evening of the 21st of July that Frundsberg arrived with his following. On his side, Frundsberg knew Schneider and other of the peasant leaders, and he and Truchsess agreed to effect their purpose, if possible, through the treachery of these men. The subordinate leaders were won over by Walter Bach, and a secret meeting was arranged at which a large sum of money was handed to the traitors. A signal having been agreed upon, they returned to the insurgent camp and persuaded the peasants to leave their strong position on the pretext that it was impossible to attack the combined forces from it! Truchsess immediately opened a heavy cannonade against the peasant position, which gave Bach the opportunity of setting fire, without being suspected, to the kegs containing the store of powder.

There were now three contingents massed on the Luibas, on the opposite side to Truchsess's camp. Two of these were commanded respectively by Schneider and Bach, and the third was under Knopf von Luibas, who was not in the conspiracy. The two traitors had bribed the keepers of the ordnance to leave it behind, whilst they marched out with their following. This occurred at midnight. No sooner had they reached open ground than the whole forces of the League were heard approaching. The unexpected move caused a sudden panic. Companies got into confusion and began to disperse in all directions, the peasants seeking cover in the neighbouring valleys, and woods. Meanwhile, the guilty leaders had fled, and gained Swiss territory within a few days. The whole ordnance fell into the hands of the League's forces.

But the victory was not quite complete, since the contingent led by Knopf von Luibas, unaware of what was taking place, held together. When, at daybreak, it was perceived treachery had been at work and that the two contingents had melted away, Knopf and his men hurriedly withdrew and managed to safely reach a good position on a hill above the town of Kempten. Truchsess, who could not attack them there, adopted the tactics of surrounding the hill with a sea of fire, caused by the conflagration of more than two hundred villages and homesteads. Numbers of women and children and old people perished in these fires. At the same time, the horsemen of the League occupied all outlets. As the result, the peasants were on the point of being starved out.

Finally they were compelled to surrender, and descended into the hostile camp with the usual white staves in their hands. The conditions exacted were a fresh oath of allegiance, a tribute of six gulden from every hearth, and a further indemnity to their lords, the amount to be decided by the Swabian League, which should also be the arbiter in all disputes between them and their lords. Truchsess immediately had eighteen leaders executed, besides others later on-in all some thirty persons. Knopf himself, with some other leaders, escaped. He was seized later on. however, in Bregenz, and, with a comrade named Kunzwirth, hanged after a long imprisonment.

Truchsess now threw strong garrisons into the towns of Kempten and Kaufbeuren, to overawe the country-folk. Thus ended the peasant revolt in the districts of Upper Swabia.

In the meantime, Duke Antoine of Lorraine had arrived with a large force of local men-at-arms, together with German and Italian mercenaries and others, intent on suppressing the peasant insurrection in Elsass. With these troops he pressed through the Vosges and appeared before Zabern, where Erasmus Gerber had fixed his camp. On the 17th of May, a body of peasants that had come to the relief of the main force in Zabern was defeated and driven back into the village of Lipstein, which was surrounded and burnt. This was not effected without some hard fighting. There was a desperate struggle for the position. Several times the attack was renewed, until the ducal army was finally successful in penetrating through the peasant stockade into the village. The church now became the citadel of the defenders. Flames then burst out on all sides, eventually reaching the defenders themselves. The latter, seeing their case to be hopeless, begged for grace, but it was too late. They rushed from the flames only to be mercilessly run through in the streets and lanes of the village. The accounts of the numbers slain vary between 2,000 and 6,000.

Amongst the mercenaries employed by the duke were Albanians, Stratiots, and possibly others from eastern Europe. These contributed an element of cold-blooded butchery which was not to be found amongst the Germans even of that age. Children of eight, ten and twelve were ruthlessly killed. Women and girls were dragged through the corn, ravished, and butchered. News of these things caused a panic throughout all the surrounding territory, and thirty waggons containing women and children from the neighbouring villages presented themselves the same evening at the gates of Kochersberg, a town belonging to Strasburg.

The occurrence naturally had its effect upon Zabern itself which surrendered. Next morning the peasants opened the gates, and under the solemn promise of mercy from the duke they streamed out without their arms but with the necessary tokens of submission — the white staves in their hands. The account of what followed is here quoted from Hardtfelder (Geschichte des Bauernkriegs in Siidwest-Deutschland, p.130 sqq). "The free-lances of the duke accompanied the exodus of the peasants. Suddenly there arose a quarrel between a free-lance and a peasant, the latter defending himself because, as the report says, he feared to be robbed of his money. Volleyr also relates that the peasants had irritated the soldiers by the cry of 'Long live Luther!' Suddenly the shout was heard 'Strike! It is allowed us!' Thereupon began a frightful massacre. The freelances struck down the defenceless peasants, who sought to reach the town by precipitate flight. The majority, however, were despatched before they got there; the free-lances simultaneously with the fugitives pressed into the town, although Count Salm with his horsemen tried to prevent this. The slaughter was here continued, not only the peasants who were in the town being murdered, but the greater portion of the citizens sharing their fate. Those peasants who had sought to flee from the town in other directions fell into the hands of the Lorrainers and were killed. Still worse would have happened, if the princes had not at this time hurried up and stopped further mischief. The Geldrian mercenaries, who had plundered Zabern, would have set fire to the whole town had they not been prevented. Even the wounded had now to be spared, and the inhabitants also escaped if they fastened on themselves the cross of Lorraine."

So great was the number of the slain that the roads leading to the town were strewn with corpses, and it was hardly possible to enter the gates for the heaps of dead that lay there. From sixteen to twenty thousand peasants were slain on this occasion.

The brutal Bavarian chancellor, Leonhard von Eck, reports on the 27th of May, that the duke had destroyed 20,000 peasants, and adds that so many peasants lay unburied that "to write with modesty, the self-same dead have so stunk that many women who fled from the country did leave their children untended; the which, therefore, did perish of hunger". He continues: "The said duke hath on Saturday slain a band of four thousand peasants, and now turneth against other bands who in the same place are rebellious, so that it bethinketh me that he will make a wilderness of the length of the whole Rhine".

The Duke Antoine treated the campaign as a kind of religious crusade against the new Lutheran doctrines. There is some doubt as to his guilt as regards the treacherous massacre of Zabern. Whether it was carried out by his positive orders or not, it is sufficiently clear that no adequate measures were taken to prevent the heterogeneous elements of his army from getting beyond control.

The ducal forces raged, slaughtering and plundering, throughout Elsass. Heavy ransoms and tributes were everywhere exacted from the towns and villages that had taken part in the insurrection. Everywhere feudal homage had to be made anew. The peasants were again forced under the old yokes, the original dues and corvées being exacted from then. In many places they were forbidden the right of assembly and of bearing any arms except the short dagger. Indemnity was insisted upon for the religious houses plundered. Oftentimes they had to hand over any charters or written concessions they might have previously obtained from their feudal superiors.

In Baden, the Austrian Government at Ensisheim showed itself merciless in the punishment of all who had taken any prominent share in the rebellion. So numerous were the executions that, playing on the name of the town, people were wont to say that it was indeed "the home of the sword" — Ensis-heim. Curiously enough the peasants, when the insurrection was at its height, do not seem to have made any serious attempt to capture this small township, the seat of the Hapsburg power in the country, although they without doubt threatened it on more than one occasion. This is the more remarkable seeing that Ensisheim is situated on a plain, and hence is easy of access, and that the walls, the ruins of which I have carefully examined, were exceptionally thin and could hardly have sustained themselves long, even against the rough and imperfect ordnance at the disposal of the peasant forces.

It is interesting to note that on the manor of Stühlingen, the territory of Count Georg von Lupfen, where the movement, according to tradition, first began, in the autumn of 1524, the peasants succumbed and were brought again under the yoke early in July. The only concession they seem to have obtained was the curious one of freedom of the chase of bears and wolves, which would seem to indicate that these animals were common at that time in the district. All other objects of the chase were prohibited to the peasants. The new religious doctrines were forbidden to be preached. A ransom of six gulden per hearth was enforced. The tocsins or alarm-bells on the church towers, which in so many places had given the signal for the rising, were ordered to be removed. Every form of combination was suppressed.

At the same tune the movements along the lake of Constance collapsed. The peasants of the Hegau, as it was called, after Truchsess's retreat into Würtemberg, before the battle of Böblingen, had carried on a bitter conflict with the garrisons of the towns Stockach and Zell. The latter set several villages on fire, and committed such atrocities as the burning of women and children.

Count Felix von Werdenberg, who had repturned from Italy at the same time as Frundsberg with a force of mercenaries and others, attacked the peasants on the 16th of July at Hilzingen, the place where the great "church-ale" was held in October, 1524, at which the movement of the district was consolidated. Here, too, the peasants were totally defeated, and the revolt perished in slaughter and flight. Radolfzell was relieved, and the besieging force was scattered. The greatest of the peasant leaders in south-western Germany, Hans Müller von Bulgenbach, was seized and beheaded.

Later on, one of his colleagues, Conrad Jehle, was captured and hanged upon the nearest oak tree without form of trial. This took place on the lands of the Abbey of St. Blasien in the Black Forest, which he had spared when it was in the power of his followers. One morning the right hand of his corpse was found nailed to the great gate of the abbey, with the words "This hand will avenge itself" scrawled underneath, evidently the writing of one of Jehle's faithful adherents. A short time afterwards the buildings of the wealthy foundation burst into flame one night, and in a few hours the massive pile was a heap of ruins. The cause of the fire was never ascertained.

The Archduke Ferdinand would like to have punished with the usual brutality those bands of the Breisgau district which had forced the town of Freiburg into their brotherhood. But the peasants of the Sundgau and the Klettgau, who had also assisted in the matter, had appealed to the Swiss to take them into their hands. The Baselers did not seem unwilling to listen to their proposal, and offered them at all events their friendly offices as mediators. They appear to have threatened both sides that they would interfere with the recalcitrant party if a compromise were rejected. The military repute of the Swiss, which, in spite of the defeat of Marignano ten years before, was still sufficiently great to make even the archduke pause before driving matters to extremities.

Negotiations were entered into with the insurgents, which were concluded on the 18th of September by the treaty of Offenburg, by which the peasants agreed to accept provisions reinstating their lords in their old rights as to dues and services, and fixing a sum as indemnity for damage done and a fine of six gulden for every hearth. But, although compelled by the force of circumstances to accept these terms, the Breisgau and Sundgau peasants were by no means cowed. "Erzwungener Eid ist Gott leid," or, as we may translate it, "Forced oaths God loathes," said they. They made no secret of their intention to rebel again as soon as the archduke's men-at-arms should have left the land. So threatening did they become that the town of Freiburg had to demand of the Austrian authorities a standing force of three hundred men to overawe the countryside throughout the ensuing winter.

The most favourable conditions of all were obtained by the peasants on the lands of the humane Markgraf Philip of Baden, who granted some notable ameliorations in their condition. He had done his best to obtain favourable conditions for those on his brother's and others' territories.

The town of Waldshut, one of the earliest centres of the rebellion, held out against its Austrian masters long after the surrounding country had been completely subdued. But on the 12th of December it, too, was taken and suffered the usual pains and penalties. A short time before, Balthaser Hubmayer, the revolutionary preacher, whom the citizens had welcomed with such transports in the spring of the year, succeeded in escaping, but it was only to meet a death at the stake, in Vienna, four years later, as an Anabaptist.

Let us now cast a retrospective glance at the course of the Civil War. We have seen that the rebellion, which had carried all before it with a few noteworthy exceptions, from its beginning up to the second week in May, thenceforward underwent defeat after defeat. The first of these irreparable disasters, the battle of Böblingen, took place on the 12th of May. This meant practically the end of the movement in Würtemberg. Three days afterwards occurred the overthrow of the revolt in Thuringia and the neighbouring countries, effected by the fatal blow dealt the peasant forces at Frankenhausen. The capture and massacre of Zabern, which followed two days later, was the decisive event in Duke Antoine's campaign against the peasants of the far-off lands of the extreme south-west. Then came the battle of Königshofen on the 2nd of June, a disaster which delivered the Franconian movement into the hands of the Swabian League and its allies. It was not before the end of July that treachery dissolved the powerful contingents massed on the Luibas in Upper Swabia. But by this time the movement throughout those countries which in the present day constitute the new German Empire was to all intents and purposes crushed. "Military operations," as the modern phrase goes, were continued in special districts throughout August, and it was not indeed before the middle of September that the last sparks of the active revolt were trodden out.

The fact is, that as long as the German territories were denuded of fighting men, and as long as the only resistance the peasant bands met with was the small force under Truchsess, which was all the Swabian League could then muster, and which could obviously only be in one place at one time, the insurrection naturally had things all its own way. The case was very different when large bodies of knights, mercenaries, and men-at-arms of all descriptions began to troop back from Italy on the termination of the Italian campaign after the imperial victory at Pavia. The inability of raw peasant levies to successfully encounter trained fighting men — their superiors alike in experience, organisation and equipment, was immediately apparent. The demoralising influence of drink, gluttony and general laxness, which was so much in evidence amongst the peasant hands, was, of course, a contributory cause of the rapid extinction of the movement, but even apart from this, as we have elsewhere pointed out, the case was hopeless.

Hangings, beheadings and slaughter were at last too much even for the palate of the governing classes, and at the Reichstag, held at the end of August, a rescript was issued urging mercy and forbearance upon the lords of the soil, deprecating fresh impositions or undue exactions, and even going so far as to threaten that those lords who acted in a contrary sense might find themselves refused imperial assistance when in need. For in spite of the discomfiture he had suffered, the "common man" had by no means even yet lost all hope. A belief in the possibility of speedily renewing the rising was active amongst the peasantry throughout the winter of 1525 and the spring of 1526, and this hope did not at the time seem altogether groundless. There was, indeed, amidst the general wilderness of disaster, one oasis in which the peasant was still holding his own, and was even scoring some relatively lasting successes. In the archbishopric of Salzburg the insurgents were still practically the masters of the situation. In Tyrol, under the chief leadership of the most able, and many-sided genius of the whole insurrection, Michael Gaismayr, the peasants had extorted noteworthy concessions from their feudal lord, the arch-duke, at the Landtag opened by him at Innsbruck on the 15th of June. In the neighbouring territories, moreover, the rebels were still active. With events in these Austrian lands we shall deal in the following chapter.

Notes

1. Amongst the curiosities of literature may be included the translation of the title of this manifesto by Prof. T. M. Lindsay, D.D., in the Encyclopaedia Britannica, 9th Edition (Article, "Luther"). The German title is "Wider die morderischen und rauberischen Rotten der Bauern". Prof. Lindsay's translation is "Against the murdering, robbing Rats (sic) of Peasants"!

2. The above is the traditional account accepted by Zimmermann and other authorities. Wilhelm Blos and some recent investigators have, however, unearthed statements in contemporary documents which place the matter in a different light. An old chronicle of the time states: "On the 9th of June, Florian Geyer was stabbed on the field near Rimpar". It is suggested that the theory that he fell near Schwabisch-Hall was caused by a badly-written manuscript. Florian, it is said, fled to the castle near Rimpar of the knight Grumbach, to whose sister, Barbara, he was betrothed. This Grumbach is alleged to have caused Florian to be treacherously murdered by one of his servants in a wood as he rode away from the castle. The story is expressly confirmed in a pamphlet issued by the Bishop of Würzburg against Grumbach, when some years later he was at feud with him: "It is the certain truth that Grumbach, a man of evil fame, did cause in the Peasants War a nobleman named Florian Geyer, who had lodged with him in his house, to be pierced through by one of his servants by his command in a wood, called the Gramschatz Wood. And, albeit that this murder be now somewhat forgotten of the younger people, yet are there many old and worthy persons to whom it is not hidden, but who are much mindful thereof."

Chapter IX. The Alpine Glow in the Austrian Territories.

The revolt in Styria (Steuermarck) which Sigsmund Dietrichstein had partially suppressed, broke out again later on. Encouraged from Vienna, Dietrichstein glutted himself with the most monstrous exactions and cruelties. All the districts where the revolt had sprung up were condemned to ruinous tribute and ransom money. In addition to this, impaling, flaying and quartering constituted the order of the day with him. His mercenaries amused themselves with cutting off the breasts of the peasant women and ripping open the abdomens of those about to become mothers. So at last the cup was filled to overflowing. The town of Schladming, on the border of the Salzburg territory, had yielded to Dietrichstein. Seeing the situation, the united contingent of the Styrian and Salzburg peasants sent a demand to the town to enter the "Christian Brotherhood". Dietrichstein, on being informed of this, proceeded to the township with a force which he disposed partly inside the walls and partly before them outside. He then proceeded to enter into negotiations with the peasants, being, of course, on treachery intent. Suddenly, on the morning of the 3rd of July, the alarm was given that the enemy was approaching. On showing himself at the window of the inn where he was lodging, he was struck by a missile. He succeeded, however, in rushing downstairs anti mounting his horse, and with two hundred followers he gained the place where fighting was going on. His horse was stabbed under him, and he himself received a blow on the head. By his side other knights fell. But now most of the men he had about him deserted to the peasants. The rest of the knights fled and entrenched themselves in the church, Dietrichstein himself surrendering to his own mutinous free-lances. By a surprise, a body of about four thousand peasants had overpowered the camp outside the town, and had become possessed of its ordnance and ammunition. The horsemen had fled in a panic. Of the Bohemian mercenaries, some escaped and some were made prisoners. Numbers were killed or driven into the stream. The town opened its gates after three thousand of Dietrichstein's force were killed, amongst them a large number of Carinthian and Styrian nobles. Eighteen knights were taken in the church alone.

The prisoners of rank were brought into the peasant camp, Dietrichstein amongst them. A ring was formed, and the whole body of peasants was called together to give judgment. The captain of the baronial forces was brought forward, and a formal accusation of all his crimes was entered against him. A demand was made that he should be impaled. On the matter being put to the vote, the whole four thousand hands were held up in favour of the execution. Dietrichstein pleaded the promise of knightly treatment he had obtained from the free-lances. Thereupon a dissension arose between the latter and the peasants, and eventually the matter was referred to the peasant council sitting at Salzburg. Here again, dissension seems to have arisen between the council and the maim body of the insurgents assembled in the town. The council wrote recommending honourable captivity for the noble prisoners. The general assembly, on the contrary, sent a letter demanding their execution.

A compromise is stated to have been effected in the camp outside Schladming, by which the Bohemian and other foreigners, noble and otherwise, were beheaded in the market-place of the town. The German nobles, on the other hand, including Dietrichstein, were spared, but had to suffer every imaginable contumely from their captors. They were stripped of their knightly raiment and dressed in peasant clothes. Peasant hats were put upon their heads, and they were led away on waggon-horses to the castle of Werfen, already occupied by the insurgents. The peasants found in the town all the money which Dietrichstein had amassed through his impositions, besides considerable property belonging to the imprisoned nobles.

After these events the Schladming contingent proceeded to take steps to renew the insurrection throughout Styria. In Carinthia and the Austrian hereditary dominions an agreement had been come to between the peasants and their lords. The smaller nobles and the townships in fact, in many cases, had themselves urged a general reduction of the burdens of the "common man". They were lenient as regarded ransom-money, in spite of the representations of the archduke. The leaders fled into the Salzburg territory.

In the Landtag at Innsbruck the archduke had succeeded in pacifying the greater part of his own Duchy of Tyrol. He had abolished many grievances, and had fixed the next Landtag to be held at Bozen. The concessions which Ferdinand accorded the Tyrolese were in fact sufficiently remarkable to lend colour to the supposition that he had a sentimental affection for his patrimonial province. Amongst other things, a complete amnesty was granted. Gaismayr, however, does not seem to have been at all satisfied with the result. As we have already seen, he looked farther than the mere alleviation of the feudal yoke. He had meanwhile resigned the leadership, but his followers were not inactive. Two of them were zealously preaching at Meran and Sterzing, and inveighing against the decisions of the Landtag. Several of the rural communities refused to give their assent, and organised themselves anew, notably in the Brixen territories. Having appointed leaders, they formed themselves into a contingent and marched upon Trient, which town they bombarded.

About sixteen thousand men were got together to suppress the revolt. By the end of September it was completely crushed, several of the leaders being executed, and the rest fleeing, mostly into Venetian territory, which at this time furnished a refuge for numbers of the archduke's rebellious subjects. In Trient and the surrounding district the repression was frightful. The current forms of torture were ruthlessly applied — mutilation, quartering, impaling and roasting alive. Some, according to the contemporary chronicle, had their hearts cut out and suspended round their necks. Every prisoner was branded on the forehead before being dismissed. Numbers, however, succeeded in escaping into Italy.

Gaismayr was meanwhile arrested and brought to Innsbruck. He was at first liberated on parole, but, finding that the authorities neglected to carry out the accepted decisions of the Landtag and were everywhere shedding the blood of the peasants, he probably thought himself absolved from his oath, and accordingly, at the end of September, he sought refuge in flight. He threatened that, should he be molested, he had eighteen townships and villages sworn to defend him.

Meanwhile the movement in Salzburg went on apace. As we have seen, Duke Wilhelm of Bavaria was not displeased at the uncomfortable position of his feudal neighbour, the Archbishop of Salzburg. Indeed, he let the insurgents clearly understand that his emissaries were sent merely to mediate and not to intimidate. The Bavarian chancellor, the stern old aristocrat Leonhard von Eck, opposed this policy of his master, which threatened at one time to bring about a serious conflict between the Bavarian Wittelsbachs and the Austrian Hapsburgs, but which in the long run came to nothing. When, towards the end of June, the Swabian League, in response to the urgent representations of the archbishop, claimed Bavarian assistance for the suppression of the Salzburg rebels, the duke succeeded it: postponing the day of decision. It was thus not until the end of August that the terms of peace were arranged, by which the old dues and corvées were to be re-established, indemnification made for loss sustained by the rebellion, and a fine of 14,000 gulden paid to the Swabian League. An amnesty was granted, and the Swabian League was to decide the villeins' claims against their lords. But ominous threatenings were still heard that "so soon as the bushes should be green they would be rid of nobles and gentlemen". The

Duke of Bavaria had thus to be satisfied with effecting what proved little more than an armistice. In fact, the peasants had shown themselves more than a match for the League's troops sent against them under Frundsberg in conjunction with the reluctant assistance of the Bavarian duke.

As a result of the treaty, the nobles detained in the castle of Werfen were released, and the archbishop, who for months had been besieged in his fortress above Salzburg, was, of course, once more free. But the remembrance of the defeat at Schladming still rankled in the breasts of the Archduke Ferdinand and the nobles. The peasants were indeed magnanimous enough in their treatment of their captives, notably of Dietrichstein, from whom they had suffered so much.(1) But this did not satisfy the authorities and territorial lords, who thought that they ought to have a monopoly of killing. Accordingly, in the midst of the peace, Count Salm with a company: of free-lances swept down upon the town and fired it on all sides. The wretched inhabitants rushing out were hurled back into the flames, without regard to age or sex. Large numbers of peasants in the neighbourhood of Schladming were hanged from the trees. The town itself was reduced to a heap of ashes. This dastardly and bloodthirsty act of treachery excited the peasants anew. Finally, about the middle of October, the countrymen once more met together near the town of Radstadt, and drew up a remonstrance against the archbishop's multitudinous breaches of the treaty, and against the atrocities committed by the imperial troops, presumably at the instance of the archduke.

Similar assemblies were held in other places, and communications were entered into with the Brixen district of Tyrol, special use being made of the great "church-ale" of the town of Brixen itself. But the inhabitants were disinclined for the moment to break the treaty they had entered into with their bishop, and in fact the revolt did not burst into renewed activity until early in the following year.

Meanwhile Michael Gaismayr had escaped into Switzerland, visiting Zurich, Luzern, and parts of Graubünden, and entering into relations with the numerous refugees from South Germany and elsewhere then in the Swiss cantons. In Chur he was seen, it was alleged, in company with an emissary of the French court. Francis I. was at this time in league with Venice to secretly further the rebellion in the Alpine districts, with a view of harassing his enemy Charles V. He was now, it is true, a prisoner in the hands of the latter, but his policy was, of course, being carried on by his representatives. Towards the end of the winter, Gaismayr took up his abode at Taufers, on the Tyrolese frontier of Appenzell, whence he endeavoured to stir up a revolt in order to seize some of the Bishop of Chur's ordnance in the neighbourhood. This plan, however, miscarried.

In the beginning of January, 1526, he issued a manifesto containing the objects for which the Tyrolese were to rise. The first demand was the destruction of all the godless, who persecuted the true word of God and oppressed the "common man". Pictures, masses and shrines were to be abolished. The walls and towers of the towns, together with all castles and strongholds, were to be levelled with the ground. Henceforth, there were to be only villages, to the end that complete equality might obtain. Each year magistrates were to be chosen by the popular voice, who were to hold court every Monday. All the judicial authorities were to be paid for out of the common treasury. A central government was to be chosen by the whole country and a university established at Brixen, three members of which were to be appointed as permanent assessors to the government. Dues and rents were to be done away with; the tithe was to be retained, but applied to the support of the Reformed Church and of the poor. The monasteries were to be turned into hospitals and schools. The breeding of cattle was to be improved and the land irrigated. Oil-trees, saffron, vines and corn were to be everywhere planted. There was to be a public inspection of wares to ensure their quality and reasonable price. Usury and debasement of the coinage were to be punished. The mines were to become the property of the whole land. Passes, roads, bridges and rivers were to be kept in order by the public authority and suitable measures taken for the defence of the country against external foes.

Such is the main substance of the manifesto which the messengers of Michael Gaismayr now distributed in the valleys of western Tyrol. The ink with which he had written it was scarcely dry before news arrived of the resuscitation, in the archiepiscopal territories of Salzburg, of the movement of the previous autumn. In a few days, Gaismayr was on his wary to the seat of the struggle. Arrived there, he soon became practically the head of the movement, and later on its recognised commander, whilst his friends, most of whom he had brought with him, became his lieutenants. The miners, however, remained quiet. In fact, two companies, composed partly of miners and partly of handicraftsmen, were enrolled by the archbishop and induced to march against their peasant brethren. They were, however, defeated by the rebels.

Radstadt, a town on the frontier of Salzburg and the Austrian hereditary lands, Styria and Carinthia, was besieged by Gaismayr on the 1st of May, 1526. The capture of this town was important alike from its strategic position and from its possession of some of the best ordnance at the disposal of Archduke Ferdinand. The latter, of' hearing of Gaismayr's operations, immediately sent reinforcements to relieve Radstadt. The Swabian League also sent a small force. Gaismayr, however, as a good strategist, had taken the precaution of blocking the main roads leading to the beleaguered town. Amidst rain and sleet, the forces of the authorities with difficulty traversed the rough mountain roads, but before they were half to Radstadt they were fallen upon by a large body of peasants in a narrow defile, and out of a force of more than a thousand less than two hundred escaped.

On the 14th of June, Gaismayr's men defeated with heavy loss eight companies of the Swabian League's best fighting men. They fled in confusion, and were pursued nearly to the gates of Salzburg. Three days later, the remainder, suffered as heavy a loss in a storm on a mountain pass. But the League continued to send reinforcements, and on the 3rd of July they gained their first victory in these districts, which cost the peasants six hundred men.

Meanwhile, Gaismayr pressed closer and closer the siege of Radstadt. He stormed the town three times, but without result. At length, he found himself borne down upon from three sides by the forces of the League and of Count Salm, accordingly, he was compelled to raise the siege, and retired hurriedly but in perfect order, with a considerable body of men, first to his former camp a little way from the town and then over a pass into the Pusterthal. But Frundsberg, with three thousand mercenaries of the League, followed close upon his heels, and eventually overtook him, and the insurgent leader's contingent was forced to make its way over the passes into Venetian territory. He himself with a following reached Venice, where he received a pension of four hundred ducats, and where, it is said, he lived like a cardinal for some time.

Thus ended the campaign which Michael Gaismayr had entered upon so full of hope. Indeed the genius of this remarkable man had given this last episode in the peasant rising — this afterglow in the Alpine lands — a reasonable probability of success which scarcely any previous enterprise of the "common man" had possessed. He had, however, taken steps to negotiate with the French and Venetians with a view to military assistance, and, although his allies failed him so far as active support was concerned, the credit belongs to him of a more far-sighted diplomacy than was exhibited by any of the other leaders of the movement. His plan was for a simultaneous rising in the Salzburg district, in Tyrol and in Upper Swabia, and the failure of this plan was not due to any want of energy on his part.

"The nobleman of Etschland," as Michael was called, had a brother, Hans Gaismayr, living in a good position at Sterzing, equally enthusiastic and with unlimited confidence in his relative. Unfortunately this brother, without having succeeded in raising the district, was captured by the Austrian authorities at Sterzing, and brought to Innsbruck on the 9th of April, where he was cruelly tortured and afterwards drawn and quartered as a traitor. That this incident made Michael more unbending in his vow of destruction to all nobles may well be imagined. Indeed, until his death his name was one of terror to the constituted authorities.

In Venice, Gaismayr continued to gather up the threads of his relations alike with the popular leaders and with the agents of the more powerful states, and the prospect, in spite of the heavy discomfiture of the "common man" throughout the German territories, seemed by no means hopeless. On the contrary, from many points of view the signs of success appeared more promising than in the period just passed through of the great spontaneous but ill-organised and badly-disciplined upheaval of the peasantry and poor townsmen. For the Protestant districts and principalities were now becoming alarmed at the turn things were taking. There was a growing feeling that an attempt would be made by the victorious feudal lords, still mainly Catholic and inspired by the archduke and the chief ecclesiastical princes, to crush Lutheranism itself. A commanding personality — a strong man in the Carlylean sense — had at last appeared in the person of Gaismayr. In addition, was there not "the Man of Twiel," Duke Ulrich, secure in his powerful stronghold on the Swiss frontier of Würtemberg? Was he not surrounded by numbers of refugees, including many of the local leaders of the late movement, who had fled thither? Was he not simply waiting his opportunity to march into his hereditary dominions with a force sufficient to defy the imperial power, and to re-establish himself as Würtemberg's master at Stuttgart?

Meanwhile, on the collapse of the Tyrol movement, consequent upon the retreat of Gaismayr, the usual policy of ferocious and bestial oppression combined with treachery was pursued. An appearance of moderation was affected in the treatment of the first batch of insurgents who surrendered. They were merely required to give up their arms and to pay a fine of eight gulden per hearth. An appeal was then made to those who had not yet given in their submission to appear on a specified day at Radstadt. The seeming clemency enticed large numbers to offer themselves on the day in question. On the peasants having assembled at the town gate, the nobles rode out at the head of a body of horse and foot. One of their number then addressed the unarmed people, descanting on the sin of rebellion against their lords. This ended, a list of twenty-seven names was read out, and those who bore them were ordered to come forward. Four executioners at the same time appeared, and proceeded to strike off the heads of the designated twenty-seven leaders. The remainder of those present were compelled to take their old oath of allegiance and obedience before they were allowed to return home. The houses of those known to have taken a prominent part in the rebellion, who now either were executed or had fled, were pulled down, and painted posts were set up in their place. Small towns were degraded to the rank of villages, and the alarm-bells were torn down from the church towers.

The two towns of Radstadt and Zell, which had closed their gates and resolutely resisted the followers of Gaismayr, were, on the other hand, rewarded with special privileges. They were accorded the right of making, every Whit Monday, a procession round the high altar of the cathedral of St. Ruprecht at Salzburg during vespers and there sinking the songs of their district. The same evening, they were to be entertained from the archbishop's cellar and kitchen, the cathedral canons and the courtiers taking part. On the Tuesday after St. Vitus's Day, they, might hang their flag from the Rathhaus, and also received a gift of wine from the archiepiscopal cellars, besides being allowed to fish in the preserved streams of their feudal overlord.

Throughout the year 1527, especially in the early summer, the whole Catholic feudal world was filled with dread at the return of Gasmayr to revivify the suppressed movement, perhaps with a French and Venetian understanding and the co-operation or benevolent neutrality of some at least of the Protestant states. The peasants, the small townsmen, and the Protestant sectaries generally were correspondingly hopeful. The Alpine lands were looked toward on the one side with fear and on the other with joyful expectation as the hearth and refuge of popular freedom. Through the whole of central and southern Germany the name of the great peasant leader from Tyrol became in every village a household word. Free-lances back from serving in the recent campaigns spoke in terms of unconcealed admiration for the valiant commander against whom they had been fighting. In the public room of many a hostelry the deeds of Michael Gaismyr, and the chances of his return to head a larger movement than the one just defeated, were eagerly discussed.

Various were the reports as to his probable action. It was said at one time that he was about to proceed from Venetian territory to Trient, and thence by forced marches into the Tyrol valleys, to call the people to arms under the protection of the Venetian Republic and its allies, who would thereby secure a free hand against Charles V. In other directions. But time passed on and yet there was no invasion from the south. Finally, in the early spring of 1528, Gaismayr was reported to have been seen in Switzerland, particularly in Zurich. The rumour was confirmed, and it further became known that he had received the citizenship of this canton, and that he was regarded as plenipotentiary for the Venetian Republic, in which capacity he was negotiating with Count Ulrich of Würtemberg, with the reformed Swiss cantons, and with other powerful Protestant interests in Germany. It was believed that he had, in short, in his hands the threads of a strong combination against the emperor. Certain it was that extensive recruitings in various districts, especially in Graubünden, were being made in his name.

By the middle of June; the matter had so far taken definite shape that it was reported that several thousand Swiss were already on the march to join Gaismayr in the mountain passes leading to Austria, and that the intention was to invade his native Etschland. This last report was not true, and it is difficult now to say precisely how far the negotiations for an anti-imperial league had proceeded, but that there were such there is no doubt. We may reasonably suppose that affairs were in train by August, 1528, when news arrived of Charles's victory at Naples on the 19th of that month, and the parties concerned seemed to have lost heart, the scheme coming to nothing in a few weeks. Ferdinand and his councillors had already set a price on Gaismayr's head. One of his followers was bribed to murder him. The man took the money, but omitted his part of the bargain. The Bishop of Brixen now also adopted the assassination policy, but still no German-speaking man was forthcoming to carry it out. At last, two wretched Spanish bravos expressed their readiness for a large sum in gold to undertake the crime. They repaired to Padua, in the Venetian territory, whither Gaismayr had returned, and one night, breaking into his apartment whilst he was asleep, they stabbed him to the heart, subsequently severing his head from his body. The head was then carefully preserved and brought by the assassins to the archduke at Innsbruck. Shortly afterwards, Gaismayr's chief lieutenant, a brave man named Pässler, was murdered by one of his own followers, also bribed to the deed by the Austrian Court. The money was again in this case handed over on the receipt of the head at Innsbruck.

All prospects were now gone, for the time being, for the popular movement. The terror of the Catholic feudal estates and the hope of the "common man," Michael Gaismayr, was dead. The other leaders were dispersed in exile or killed or imprisoned, save for a few who remained with Duke Ulrich in the "Hohentwiel ". The duke himself was to regain his patrimony of Würtemberg, but not as he at one time imagined by the aid of the peasants ostensibly fighting for their own rights. In short, with Gaismayr's death the afterglow of the Peasants War finally faded away. The revolt of the "common man" had been extinguished.

Notes

1. Indeed, if we may believe a recent authority, the story of the executions by the peasants on Schladming marketplace is a historical fable. (Krones apud Janssen, vol. ii., p.571, note).

Chapter X. Conclusion.

IN the foregoing pages we have followed the chief episodes in the last great agrarian uprising of the Middle Ages. Its result was, with some few exceptions, a rivetting of the peasant's chains and an increase of his burdens. More than a thousand castles and religious houses were destroyed in Germany alone during 1525. Many priceless works of mediaeval art of all kinds perished. But we must not allow our regret at such vandalism to blind us in any way to the intrinsic righteousness of the popular demands.

Just as little should our judgment be influenced by the fact that we can now see that much of the peasant programme was out of the line of natural social progress, and that the war itself was carried on from the beginning in a manner that rendered success well-nigh impossible, if only from a military point of view. The revolt, as we have seen, was crushed piecemeal, just as it had arisen piecemeal. Co-operation there was none. Thomas Münzer found it hopeless to connect effectively the movement in the countries of Thuringia and Franconia, allied as they were in many ways. In consequence of the movements being thus territorially limited, the forces of the authorities, such as that of the Swabian League, had little difficulty in defeating the several insurgent bodies one after the other.

Of the ruthless and cold-blooded butchery which usually followed we have seen enough. The blow was indeed a heavy one for the "common man" generally, and for the peasant more especially. As to the few exceptions where something was gained, one of the most noteworthy was the case of the subjects of Count Philip of Baden, who were granted some solid ameliorations.

The attitude of the official Lutheran party towards the poor country-folk continued as infamous after the war as it had been on the first sign that fortune was forsaking their cause. Like master, like man. Luther's jackal, the "gentle" Melancthon, specially signalised himself by urging on the feudal barons with Scriptural arguments to the blood-sucking and oppression of their villeins. A humane and honourable nobleman, Heinrich von Einsiedel, was touched in conscience at the corvées and heavy dues to which he found himself entitled. He sent to Luther for advice upon the subject. Luther replied that the existing exactions which had been handed down to him from his parents need not trouble his conscience, adding that it would not be good for corvées to be given up, since the "common man" ought to have burdens imposed upon him, as otherwise he would become overbearing. He further remarked that a severe treatment in material things was pleasing to God, even though it might seem to be too harsh. Spalatin writes in a like strain that the burdens in Germany were, if anything, too light. Subjects, according to Melancthon, ought to know that they are serving God in the burdens they bear for their superiors, whether it were journeying, paying tribute, or otherwise, and as pleasing to God as though they raised the dead at God's own behest. Subjects should look up to their lords as wise and just men, and hence be thankful to them. However unjust, tyrannical and cruel the lord might be, there was never any justification for rebellion.

A friend and follower of Luther and Melancthon — Martin Butzer by name went still further. According to this "reforming" worthy, a subject was to obey his lord in everything. This was all that concerned him. It was not for him to consider whether what was enjoined was, or was not, contrary to the will of God. That was a matter for his feudal superior and God to settle between them. Referring to the doctrines of the revolutionary sects, Butzer urges the authorities to extirpate all those professing a false religion. Such men, he says, deserve a heavier punishment than thieves, robbers and murderers. Even their wives and innocent children and cattle should be destroyed (ap. Janssen, Vol. i., p.595).

Luther himself quotes, in a sermon on "Genesis," the instances of Abraham and Abimelech and other Old Testament worthies, as justifying slavery and the treatment of a slave as a beast of burden. "Sheep, cattle, men-servants and maid-servants, they were all possessions," says Luther, "to be sold as it pleased them like other beasts. It were even a good thing were it still so. For else no man may compel nor tame the servile folk" (Sammtliche Werke, xv., 276). In other discourses he enforces the same doctrine, observing that if the world is to last for any time, and is to be kept going, it will be necessary to restore the patriarchal condition. Capito, the Strassburg preacher, in a letter to a colleague, writes lamenting that the pamphlets and discourses of Luther had contributed not a little to give edge to the bloodthirsty vengeance of the princes and nobles after the insurrection.

The total number of the peasants and their allies who fell either in fighting or at the hands of the executioners is estimated by Anselm in his Berner Chronik at a hundred and thirty thousand. It was certainly not less than a hundred thousand. For months after, the executioner was active in many of the affected districts. Spalatin says: "Of hanging and beheading there is no end".

Another writer has it: "It was all so that even a stone had been moved to pity, for the chastisement and vengeance of the conquering lords was great". The executions within the jurisdiction of the Swabian League alone are stated at ten thousand. Truchsess's provost boasted of having hanged or beheaded twelve hundred with his own hand. More than fifty thousand fugitives were recorded. These, according to a Swabian League order, were all outlawed in such wise that any one who found them might slay them without fear of consequences.

The sentences and executions were conducted with true mediaeval levity. It is narrated in a contemporary chronicle that in one village in the Henneberg territory all the inhabitants had fled on the approach of the count and his men-at-arms save two tilers. The two were being led to execution when one appeared to weep bitterly, and his reply to interrogatories was that he bewailed the dwellings of the aristocracy thereabouts, for henceforth there would be no one to supply them with durable tiles. Thereupon his companion burst out laughing, because, said he, it had just occurred to him that he would not know where to place his hat after his head had been taken off. These mildly humorous remarks obtained for both of them a free pardon.

The aspect of those parts of the country where the war had most heavily raged was deplorable in the extreme. In addition to the many hundreds of castles and monasteries destroyed, almost as many villages and small towns had been levelled with the ground by one side or the other, especially by the Swabian League and the various princely forces. Many places were annihilated for having taken part with the peasants, even when they had been compelled by force to do so. Fields in these districts were everywhere laid waste or left uncultivated. Enormous sums were exacted as indemnity. In many of the villages peasants previously well-to-do were ruined. There seemed no limit to the bleeding of the "common man," under the pretence of compensation for damage done by the insurrection.

The condition of the families of the dead and of the fugitives was appalling. Numbers perished from starvation. The wives and children of the insurgents were in some cases forcibly driven from their homesteads and even from their native territory. In one of the pamphlets published in 1525 anent the events of that year, we read: "Houses are burned; fields and vineyards lie fallow; clothes and household goods are robbed or burned; cattle and sheep are taken away; the same as to horses and trappings. The prince, the gentleman, or the nobleman will have his rent and due. Eternal God, whither shall the widows and poor children go forth to seek it?" Referring to the Lutheran campaign against friars and poor scholars, beggars and pilgrims, the writer observes: "Think ye now that because of God's anger for the sake of one beggar, ye must even for a season bear with twenty, thirty, nay still more?"

The courts of arbitration, which were established in various districts to adjudicate on the relations between lords and villeins, were naturally not given to favour the latter, whilst the fact that large numbers of deeds and charters had been burnt or otherwise destroyed in the course of the insurrection left open an extensive field for the imposition of fresh burdens. The record of the proceedings of one of the most important of these courts — that of the Swabian League's jurisdiction, which sat at Memmingen — in the dispute between the prince-abbot of Kempten and his villeins is given in full in Baumann's Akten, pp. 329-346. Here, however, the peasants did not come off so badly as in some other places. Meanwhile, all the other evils of the time, the monopolies of the merchant-princes of the cities and of the trading-syndicates, the dearness of living, the scarcity of money, etc., did not abate, but rather increased from year to year. The Catholic Church maintained itself especially in the south of Germany, and the official Reformation took on a definitely aristocratic character.

According to Baumann (Akten, Vorwort, v., vi.), the true soul of the movement of 1525 consisted in the notion of "Divine justice," the principle "that all relations, whether of political, social, or religious nature, have got to be ordered according to the directions of the 'Gospel' as the sole and exclusive source and standard of all justice". The same writer maintains that there are three phases in the development of this idea, according to which he would have the scheme of historical investigation sub-divided. In Upper Swabia, says he, "Divine justice" found expression in the well-known "Twelve Articles," but here the notion of a political reformation was as good as absent.

In the second phase, the "Divine justice" idea began to be applied to political conditions. In Tyrol and the Austrian dominions, he observes, this political side manifested itself in local or, at best, territorial patriotism. It was only in Franconia that all territorial patriotism or "particularism" was shaken off, and the idea of the unity of the German peoples received as a political goal. The Franconian influence gained over the Würtembergers to a large extent, and the plan of reform elaborated by Weigand and Hipler for the Heilbron Parliament was the most complete expression of this second phase of the movement.

The third phase is represented by the rising in Thuringia, and especially in its intellectual head, Thomas Miinzer. Here we have the doctrine of "Divine justice" taking the form of a thoroughgoing theocratic scheme, to be realised by the German people.

This division Baumann is led to make with a view to the formulation of a convenient scheme for a "codex" of documents relating to the Peasants War. It may be taken as, in the main, the best general division that can be put forward, although, as we have seen, there are places where, and times when, the practical demands of the: movement seem to have asserted themselves directly and spontaneously apart from any theory whatever.

Of the fate of many of the most active leaders of the revolt, we know nothing. George Metzler disappeared, and was seen no more after the battle of Königshofen. Several heads of the movement, according to a contemporary writer, wandered about for a long time in misery, some of them indeed seeking refuge with the Turks, who were still a standing menace to imperial Christendom. The popular preachers vanished also on the suppression of the movement. The disastrous result of the Peasants War was prejudicial even to Luther's cause in south Germany. The Catholic party reaped the advantage everywhere, evangelical preachers, even, where not insurrectionists, being persecuted. Little distinction, in fact, was made in most districts between an opponent of the Catholic Church from Luther's standpoint and one from Karlstadt's or Hubmayer's. Amongst seventy-one heretics arraigned before the Austrian court at Ensisheim, only one was acquitted. The others were broken on the wheel, burnt or drowned.

Amongst the non-clerical leaders of the popular party, Friedrich Weigand alone seems to have come off scot free. Hans Flux, of Heilbron, was denounced by his own fellowcitizens, and, for the time being, driven from his native town. It cost him a hundred gold gulden to be reinstated in the rights of citizenship. Some of the heads of the peasant companies found temporary refuge in ruined castles and other out-of-the-way places. Some even became chiefs of robber bands, and were at a later date killed in conflict with the authorities. Martin Feuerbacher was imprisoned in the imperial town of Esslingen and suffered the torture several times. Owing, however, to the good repute in which he stood with certain nobles of his neighbourhood, he was after some years reinstated in his property.

There were some who were arrested ten or fifteen years later on charges connected with the 1525 revolt. Treachery, of course, played a large part, as it has done in all defeated movements, in ensuring the fate of many of those who had been at all prominent. In fairness to Luther, who otherwise played such a villainous rôle, the fact should be recorded that he sheltered his old colleague, Karlstadt, for a short time in the Augustine monastery at Wittenberg, after the latter's escape' from Rothenburg. Ehrenfried Kumpf, the iconoclast and ex-bürgermeister of Rothenburg, died of melancholy some little while after the suppression of the insurrection. The nobility of Götz von Berlichingen and his treachery to the peasants' cause did not save him from the consequences of the part he had ostensibly played. He lay for some time an imperial prisoner in one of the towers on the town wall of Nürnberg. He was subsequently released on a solemn pledge not to quit his ancestral domains, and remained a captive on his own lands for years.

Wendel Hipler continued for some time at liberty, and might probably have escaped altogether had he not entered a process against the Counts of Hohenlohe for having seized a portion of his private fortune that lay within their power. The result of his action might have been foreseen. The counts, on hearing of it, revenged themselves by accusing him of having been a chief pillar of the rebellion. He had to flee immediately, and, after wandering about for some time in a disguise, one of the features of which is stated to have been a false nose, he was seized on his way to the Reichstag which was being held at Speier in 1526. Tenacious of his property to the last, he had hoped to obtain restitution of his rights from the assembled estates of the empire. Some months later he died in prison at Neustadt.

Of the victors, Truchsess and Frundsberg considered themselves badly treated by the authorities whom they had served so well, and Frundsberg even composed a lament on his neglect. This he loved to hear sung to the accompaniment of the harp as he swilled down his red wine. The cruel Markgraf Kasimir met a miserable death not long after from dysentery, whilst Cardinal Matthaus Lang, the Archbishop of Salzburg, ended his days insane.

Of the fate of other prominent men connected with the events described, we have spoken in the course of the narrative.

The castles and religious houses, which were destroyed, as already said, to the number of many hundreds, were in most cases not built up again. The ruins of not a few of them are indeed visible to this day. Their owners often spent the sums relentlessly wrung out of the "common man" as indemnity, in the extravagances of a gay life in the free towns or in dancing attendance at the courts of the princes and the higher nobles. The collapse of the revolt was indeed an important link in the particular chain of events that was so rapidly destroying the independent existence of the lower nobility as a separate status with a definite political position, and transforming the face of society generally. Life in the smaller castle, the knight's burg, or tower, was already tending to become an anachronism. The court of the prince, lay or ecclesiastic, was attracting to itself all the elements of nobility below it in the social hierarchy. The revolt of 1525 gave a further edge to this development, the first act of which closed with the collapse of the knights' rebellion and death of Sickingen in 1523.

The knight was becoming superfluous in the economy of the body politic. The rise of capitalism, the sudden development of the world-market, the substitution of a money medium of exchange for direct barter — all these new factors were doing their work.

Obviously the great gainers by the events of the momentous year were the representatives of the centralising principle. But the effective centralising principle was not represented by the emperor, for he stood for what was after all largely a sham centralism, because it was a centralism on a scale for which the Germanic world was not ripe. Princes and margraves were destined to be the bearers of the term territorial centralisation, the only real one to which the German peoples were to attain for a long time to come. Accordingly, just as the provincial grand seigneur of France became the courtier of the French king at Paris or Versailles, so the previously quasi-independent German knight or baron became the courtier or hanger-on of the prince within or near whose territory his hereditary manor was situate.

The eventful year 1525 was truly a landmark in German history in many ways — the year of one of the most accredited exploits of Doctor Faustus, the last mythical hero the progressive races have created; the year in which Martin Luther, the ex-monk, capped his repudiation of Catholicism and all its ways by marrying an ex-nun; the year of the definite victory of Charles V. the German Emperor over Francis I. the French King, which meant the final assertion of the "Holy Roman Empire" as a national German institution; and last, but not least, the year of the greatest and the most widespread popular movement central Europe had yet seen, and the last of the mediaeval peasant risings on a large scale. The movement of the eventful year did not, however, as many hoped and many feared, within any short time rise up again from its ashes, after discomfiture had overtaken it. In 1526, as we have seen, the genius of Gaismayr succeeded in resuscitating it, not without prospect of ultimate success, in Tyrol and other of the Austrian territories. In this year, moreover, in other outlying districts, even outside German-speaking populations, the movement flickered. Thus the traveller between the town of Bellinzona in the Swiss Canton of Ticino and the Bernardino pass in Canton Graubünden may see to-day an imposing ruin, situated on an eminence in the narrow valley just above the small Italian-speaking town of Misox. This was one of the ancestral strongholds of the family, well-known in Italian history, of the Trefuzios or Trevulzir, and was sacked by the inhabitants of Misox and the neighbouring peasants in the summer of 1526, contemporaneously with Gaismayr's rising in Tyrol. A connection between the two events would be difficult to trace, and the destruction of the castle of Misox, if not a purely spontaneous local effervescence, looks like an afterglow of the great movement, such as may well have happened in other secluded mountain valleys.

With the death of Gaismayr, however, the insurrectionary party lost its last hope for the time being. Matters gradually settled down, and the agitation took a somewhat different form. The elements of revolution now became absorbed by the Anabaptist movement, a continuation primarily in the religious sphere of the doctrines of the Zwickau enthusiasts and also in many respects of Thomas Münzer. At first northern Switzerland, especially the towns of Basel and

Zurich, became the headquarters of the new sect, which, however, spread rapidly on all sides. Persecution of the direst description did not destroy it. On the contrary, it seemed only to have the effect of evoking those social and revolutionary elements latent within it which were at first overshadowed by more purely theological interests. As it was, the hopes and aspirations of the "common man" revived this time in a form indissolubly associated with the theocratic commonwealth, the most prominent representative of which during the earlier movement had been Thomas Münzer. The Anabaptist sect subsequently concentrated its main strength at Strasburg. Driven thence, Holland and north-west Germany became its chief seat, until events culminated in the drama enacted at Münster in Westphalia in 1534 with the prophet John Bockelson as its leading figure. But neither this serious attempt to realise the popular conception of the Kingdom of God on earth nor the fortunes of the Anabaptist sect in general fall within the scope of the present volume.

THE END